The Joy of Stretching

Seeking God Within

Other books by Father Peter Bowes:

᷒

The Way, the Truth and the Life:
The Autobiography of a Christian Master

Steps on the Way

Spiritual Astrology

The Radical Path

The Word Within

Sayings of a Christian Master Teacher

Love is Simple

Pearls of a Fisherman

Sermons from the Valley

Father Peter Bowes

The Joy of Stretching

Seeking God Within

Sophia Publishing

Woodstock, IL

The Joy of Stretching

First Edition

ISBN: 978-1-329-92542-7

All citations of *The Gospel as Revealed to Me* and *Notebooks*
provided with permission from:
Centro EditorialeValtortiano
I 03036 Isola del Liri (Fr) – Italia
Tel. +39 0776 807 032 – Fax +39 07776 809 789
www.mariavaltorta.com   cev@mariavaltorta.com

For information, write to:
Sophia Publishing
509 E. Kimball Ave. Woodstock, IL 60098

Cover Art: Meira Leonard

CONTENTS

EXPERIENCING THE PRESENCE OF GOD

In the beginning, God. Very little else needs to be said. If we could get how important that is, we would be in a constant state of ecstasy. Just saying the name "God" should bring us such awe and connection that our minds stop chattering and our knees bend with gratitude for the great gift of life. Have you ever silently said the name "God" inside yourself and just let the energy of your being go towards that? Our minds are staggered with the majesty and beauty of a being so powerful and yet so loving. Here we are such small creatures, so helpless in our lack of understanding, longing to know who this great Creator is. When we reach up and within ourselves, we find a vast expanse of conscious intelligence and awareness waiting for us. This vastness of God is completely conscious of us and aware of our progress. Just because we can barely see our reflection in the mirror of this vast mind does not mean this great being is not totally and thoroughly conscious of us and all of creation.

What does it mean to be created? Where does it place us in the realm of God? Are we perhaps training to take God's place? Are we supposed to have the attitude that we have to get out of this position of being dependent on God's energy? How uncomfortable is it to us that we are sustained and supported on all sides by a divine energy that is conscious of us? Have you ever thought about these things? I can't stop thinking about them. I am absorbed in these thoughts and feelings about our Father from morning until night. In the beginning, God.

God guides us in our lives, in our choices and in our thoughts and actions. All of our lives we are taught to think like people around us and we get kind of defensive about the fact that much of our teens and twenties were spent trying to think independently. As we grow, we come to the startling discovery that all of the things that we have been thinking and believing are really nothing but warmed over scraps of half baked ideas of other unenlightened people. Then we move on to the spiritual path and everything that we have thought, felt and everything we have built must come crashing down around us. We see very clearly that what we have tried to accomplish is to set up such a rigid and secure structure inside our thinking and feeling that nothing could make us doubt or cause us any insecurity. We are told to let go and let God and we have only a partial or superficial idea of what that means. It sounds like so many things in present day fashionable spirituality that it has come to mean almost nothing. We are informed that everything that we have built that God did not build will be taken down and destroyed to become compost for our future transformation. We are left a bit adrift on the sea of possibility. We can trust our teacher and move ahead into unknown territory or we can fall back on the tried and true method of safety, security, stability and stupidity. No amount of encouragement can give you faith enough to trust a process that you are not familiar with as yet. You can either trust or you can preserve yourself and your own life as best you can. You want to move on spiritually and gain those experiences that move you past doubt and fear. Now, you have to stop thinking like the world thinks and move into the unknown territory of thinking like God, Jesus and Mary thinks. Throw out all of your own ideas and give them up to God. You have to do this if you want to make a space inside yourself for the knowledge and wisdom that God has and so that you can experience what God thinks, feels and knows.

This is humiliating and will put you through many changes. It is understandable that you might feel disoriented and out of your element. You are thinking with a whole different mind and you are seeing in a whole new way. Nothing of your old life is going to make sense to you because it was not guided and you were not able to get guidance then. This is humility. Whereas before, you were lost and at sea in your own confusion, now you are beginning to know how God works and what God wants for you in your life. Remember, experience is not the same as knowledge. Knowledge can come through books or being told or hearsay. Experience can only come through direct connection with God. You have to go through something to have an experience. You can't just emote or think to have an experience. You have to go through something. So you have to dump what you have thought about yourself, others and God in order to see what God sees and what God experiences.

How many times do I hear students ask me what they need to do to change something in their lives? I have to say, that as many times as I tell them, and I usually tell them the same thing each time, they are unable to listen to the simple truth that they have to stop thinking the old thoughts and give themselves over to God. If you continue doing the same thing over and over and expect different results, you are only fooling yourself. You have to change your thinking, feeling and behaviors if you want lasting change in your life. Why not try being obedient in a meticulous way to the directions of your teacher? Try this out sometime and see what happens. Why would they try to hurt you? Do you think they want everyone to be the same? Do you think they are insecure and need everyone to think exactly alike and have the same personality? Are you out of your mind? Think, Think, Think. We want you to be reflections of God but we want you to be yourself too. We definitely pray for your transformation into sons and daughters of light. We want your healing and we definitely want you to be yourself. But we do not feel you can lead yourself in territory you haven't traveled yet. We know your real being and your soul and what you have demonstrated and expressed is usually far from your true nature as souls and divine beings. To become that and allow yourself to open and unfold enough to be a soul/Self will take a lot of dying and letting go. You can't do it yourself. You need a guide.

Don't you see? You have many levels of mistrust that have to be peeled away. Some lessons are easy to learn because they do not pierce your core and challenge you at deep levels. Some lessons are so deep and difficult that you feel like you are going to die. Each of these deaths is necessary to make sure that nothing gets in the way of God and nothing of your old self remains. You are not alone on this journey. Thousands have traveled this path before you and they know the trials, temptations and difficulties. You are not alone. But no one else can travel the path for you. Everyone walks the path alone. It is between you and your Creator. Die to your old self. Die to the illusion that you are separate from God and your brothers and sisters. Die to the idea that you must have your own way. Die to the disease of the mass mind thinking. Die to everything that isn't God in you. If you let go of yourself a little, then God can use you a little. If you give a little, you get a little. That is the Law. If you have parts of yourself that you hold sacred, then God cannot enter there. If you hold something sacred inside you that isn't God, then you have a competing god and that will be a fenced off area in your consciousness that no visitors will be permitted entrance. What are you holding onto that stuff for? What have you built that is so wonderful, so beautiful, so important that it even remotely compares to God and to God's magnificence. "Thou shall have no other God's before God." That is the first commandment. But I see some of you have very powerful lesser gods than God in your emotional and mental house. You pay homage to them because of a thousand excuses: loneliness.

You don't have the kind of mate, lover or friend you feel you deserve and so you keep these imposter gods as backup. You pay homage to them in your resentment that the one

God, your parents or your life has let you down. You deserve to reward yourself for your sufferings because God has abandoned you. You are taking the god place in your life because of your lack of faith and trust in the one true God. What would be the scariest thing God could show you about yourself? What would be the scariest thing that God could ask you to do? What could God say to cause you to run in the opposite direction? If you come up with answers to these questions you are getting very close to the areas you hold sacred and will not allow God to enter. These are special areas inside you that God has no access to. This means you are holding back and have many fears about letting go and letting God. Will God harm you? Will God be sensitive to how important some of your special little idiosyncrasies are? God is your constant ally and source of protection. God is not out to get you. God is completely conscious and loving towards you and wants only what is best for you.

Some sacred areas may be your money and possessions, not wanting them disturbed or shifted around. Another might be the area of sexuality and relationships, not wanting God's guidance on anything you do or anyone you choose. Another area that is sneakier is the area of opinions and concepts about yourself and other people. You may secretly be thinking certain things that you feel no one, even God, could know about and so it doesn't hurt anyone. But your thoughts are powerful and transmit energy in the atmosphere around you and this influences other people. These thoughts produce a vibration that congeals around you and shut down the pure energies of God. Everything matters. These so-called private thoughts and feelings you have are transmitting into the energy field around you and they make a difference. You might want to allow God to guide these and show them up for what they are. Mostly they are your false gods that you have been worshipping for many years. Subject them to God's scrutiny so that you will not be growing any more useless plants in the garden of your soul and body.

When you are living in the presence of God, you will have no worries, no fears. Relax in God's presence knowing that your every need is taken care of. It doesn't take any time. It takes you getting out of the way and just letting the movements of God guide your day, your actions, thoughts and words. When you live in the will of God, you cannot feel separate from your brothers and sisters. You will not feel that there are two distinct and opposing energies inside warring for prominence. The battle inside you will be over and you will not lack anything. The separation you once felt will linger only as a faint memory of a time in your life when you struggled and reacted to everything. Those days are gone and you begin to accept your new life without anxiety. If you still do not know the difference between your old life and your new one, you haven't left your old life yet.

You are still holding on to your precious considerations and things you have developed in you that keep you bolstered up in your pride and anger that God did not help you when you needed it. Your resentment is still the motivating force behind your persistence in preserving your picture of yourself. You spent so much time working on those defenses and you are not about to let them go without a fight. God will not interfere or storm your castle and take those defenses and weapons away from you. God waits for you to ask and invite God into your house. Then God comes in to heal, to help, to rework and refashion your life according to God's plan, God's nature and wisdom. Then all of the things in God can be accessed by you and you are fully loved. In that love, you will blossom and grow as a tree planted by the water.

HAVE IT YOUR WAY

Each of you was given an inheritance by God of being the same nature as God and capable of being a co-creator with God. You are endowed with the rights and powers of one who can design the destiny of your own life and be supported in that endeavor by the whole intelligence and benevolence of the Father who created you. You can no more refuse this gift as you can create it for yourself and so you are stuck with it. Unfortunately very few people know about this endowment and inheritance and so very few can take it very seriously or even be conscious of it. Being conscious of this great gift seems to make a tremendous difference in the quality and nature of your human life. Those who are not conscious of this inheritance can merely operate as beings in a semi fog or sleep state. They can accident into benefits and blessings without really knowing how they came about and what the mechanism is that enables them to happen. Life for them is random and blessings come to some and not to others without much rhyme or reason. Some are lucky enough to be endowed with gifts and abundance and other poor creatures are misfortuned enough to expect other less esteemed graces in life.

You can see that life as an unconscious being has its drawbacks in terms of ever hoping to understand what is going on, much less have any say over the outcome of your life. I can't recommend that life and I am not here to help you imagine it is a blessing to anyone to live like that. What I am here to tell you is that you are a conscious being, created for a particular reason. The love of a great being fashioned you and visualized your whole possibility and potential and then gave you an environment in which to realize your wishes. God in infinite wisdom formed in you a part of itself that could create and imagine just like God.

You were set adrift on the sea of life with immense capabilities and support from the Creator and were given the task of deciding what you want and how you wish to travel. The divine being who fashioned you and infused you with the breath of life thought it unwise to interfere with your decisions, so gave you free will. This free and unrestrained will in human beings was capable of deciding anything it wanted and the power of the universe, through the decision of the great Creator, makes it imperative that you have it. And God saw that it was good.

I hope you are starting to feel better about your condition as a created being now. In fact, it may be scaring some of you that you have very little idea how to navigate with all of these choices and opportunities. I hope that you realize how many choices and possibilities there are for each of you so that you respect life itself a little more profoundly than you have in the past. The choices are overwhelming to a child who wants to know everything, to experience everything. But the child chooses what is right in front of him or her and begins the vast accumulation of experiences that makes them more aware of their world. You can choose anything too. This is your right as an heir to the realm of God. You can have anything you want. You can decide to move to the right and you will move there. You can decide to gravitate towards pleasure and you will begin to arrive there. You can be afraid of something and withdraw and protect yourself from experiences like that.

There is nothing you can't have in life if you just move in the direction of experiencing it. God wired each conscious being in creation with all the power necessary in order to obtain and acquire whatever you want. This is an inalienable right of a human being. You can have what you want and in the most philosophical sense, you already have exactly what you have wanted. When people began to think themselves better than their neighbors, then the trouble started. Jealousies, anger, fear, and worry entered into the

8

human experience and comparisons and judgments proliferated. The standard for what a person could experience was determined by looking at what everyone else wanted and valued and so people competed for a limited vision of what was common acceptance among the masses. In time everyone was boiled down to a mediocre life that others could tolerate and the exceptional people were adulated or tortured.

In your early lessons on the Tree of Life, you are taught that you have to renounce the thinking of those around you. I hope you don't do that until you get a good dose of what that thinking is. That way you can make a considered choice in letting go of the way the masses think or in keeping the parts you like. When you go to a restaurant, how do you know what to order or not order unless you have tasted some of the dishes first? It is a little hit and miss, but that is the only way to learn. So you can only renounce those thoughts of the world around you that you know from experience are not sound or ennobling of your life. You reject those ideas that your experience tells you do not make sense and do not seem to help you arrive at where you want to go. We ask you to reject the thinking of the world because from our humble experience, those thoughts generate disturbance, fear, anger, pride and separation from your brothers and sisters and from your Creator. We have observed from experience that this is what those thoughts do and we have decided not to respect or want those anymore. I won't force this option on you, but in our classes we start to point out to you the various effects those thoughts and conclusions bring to you who think them.

A long time ago, I was borrowing a neighbor's lawn mower and I kept it a little longer than I should have. Then I forgot to bring it back until the neighbor needed to cut his own lawn and remembered that it was at my house. He came over quite angry that I had forgotten to return it when I said I would. I know it doesn't sound like me and usually I would never have done things that way. But here he was and I was obviously in the wrong and had to apologize for my delay in returning the item and understood if he did not want to loan me the lawnmower again. I had a choice to be angry at him for shaming me about my negligence. I could have reacted with guilt and criticized him for being petty. I could have made excuses as to why it seemed right to me to not return it and then let him react any way he wanted. I could have groveled tremendously and with false humility tried to make it up to him with apologies and other lavish gifts that would have been out of balance with the situation. I would have been able to make any of these choices or others if I wanted to. But I would have experienced the results of such choices as well. If I acted in any way contrary to consideration, it would have unleashed a chain of events that would be hard to stop until the friendship with the neighbor would be unalterably damaged by my embarrassing behavior. You see how bad things can get? According to the state of my mind, I could decide to damage forever a friendship that could easily have remained simple and open. I didn't damage it and merely apologized and brought it right out for him to take with him. I understood and accepted that the consequence of my behavior was that he would not loan me the lawnmower again and I did not venture to ask.

What does this have to do with having it your way? Each decision that you make generates other decisions and directs a flow of energy that must of necessity carry certain consequences. Everyone is under the same natural laws that God built into creation. I want you to get clearly in your mind that you are in charge of the choices you make. Those choices make a difference and will have their effect in your life. You have a right to anything you want but you will also experience the results of those choices. You can choose to go along with everything everyone else does. You can agree to everything everyone else likes and like those things too. You can think for yourself and decide based on trial and error as you begin to be one of the thoughtful ones on the planet.

I don't know about you, but I don't like living at the effect end of things. I want to live at the cause end of things. The cause end of things creates while the effect end of things just reacts to the things that happen to you. The only way to really learn is to start wanting things and wanting experiences. This means that it is your right to have things your way. How else can you learn? If you never felt that you have been able to have just what you want, then you are really missing something in life. It is just because a person starts to have things their way that they start to be able to discriminate between what they want and what they don't want. This is imperative if you are ever to grow into a spiritual adult. I am not advocating going out and raising hell because you have never felt confident enough to do that because that will be a great error on your part. But you do have to really examine whether you want something or not. If you choose a negative experience, note that you have already called it negative or have seen the results from watching other people's lives and you know intuitively that the result will be the same for you if you go there. You are permitted to learn from other people's experience because most likely the result will be the same if you do the very same thing. That is learning too. In fact, most of what you learn from your parents is what not to do because you paid attention and saw that it did no one any good to do what they did. This is not in all situations, but mostly it is true. I don't have to rob someone to know that the police are going to apprehend me. It's simple. I don't want incarceration, so I am not going to do anything that hurts another person in order to have that experience. I might get there on a vacation of sorts because of standing for something, but for certain, I won't be there because I did anyone any harm.

You can have things your way. I want you to have the things you want and to have things your way. Have the courage and determination to have a few things your way. But also have the humility to learn from them and allow others to give you some feedback on what you have created for yourself. That is healthy and real. It is sometimes sad for me to see a student pining away for an experience that they have never had. The experience they are wishing for is not wrong and doesn't hurt anyone. They just haven't had it yet and it may be the very thing that deepens them or rounds out their understanding of others. I know it is hard sometimes, but maybe you should go and have that experience. Do you have the intestinal fortitude to live with the consequences of such a decision? Are you aware that others also have the right to make decisions because of what you do? If you decide you have never had an affair and you want one, are you aware that the ending of your relationship is well within the rights of your partner and they may just decide to leave you without your say so? You see, everything you do may affect someone else and they have a right to make decisions too. You may say, as Judas did to Jesus, that Jesus had not committed certain crimes and so Jesus could not possibly have compassion on those who committed them. Judas was speaking as the adversary at this point and Jesus condemned this attitude in Judas as saying that unless Jesus went into darkness and became darkness that Jesus could not understand or have compassion on those who chose darkness. Jesus was angry at Judas for so insane a presumption. Judas was excusing his own evil behavior under the rationalization that he was learning things that would make him a better disciple. He was teaching himself and playing god. He was also accusing Jesus of not being able to understand people because Jesus hadn't fallen into the same hole Judas was in. It is easy to see how people suffer for the choices they make and to understand with compassion what the experience creates within them. You don't need to go there yourself.

Again if you are paying attention to what other people are experiencing, your choices will narrow to those things that will ennoble your life and make things better. Improvement and growth will crown your successes because your decisions will give you the experience of knowing yourself better.

In the case of a stubborn person, I recommend that you go out and get anything that you want because you would secretly resent any limitations or advice. You want things your way and wisdom supports you getting it. I know it is risky, but take a good look at it. Isn't that what you are already doing in your mind anyway? Aren't you looking after the object of your desires and already experiencing it in your mind and feelings? You may fool yourself into thinking you are depriving yourself, but in fantasy and desire you have already visualized yourself experiencing it or you wouldn't pine after it. The more stubborn you are the more you need to go out and bang your head on life experiences that will take that bull-headedness out of you. There is a God, remember. And you aren't it. You are a being with a pre-patterned nature that God knows, so it might be useful for you to refer to the owner's manual and see how you really work. That may take your ego down a notch and that would be healthy for you. Otherwise you will find yourself in the backwaters of your own confusion wondering how you managed to mess up your life. It is really simple. If you try to navigate your ship without a compass and without divine inspiration, you will be one of the shipwrecked people on the earth. But you can be thankful that you have things just the way you wanted them. Everything that happens to you, you in some way created or accepted. That is a law. That is the truth. Have it your way.

I was working with a new priest on a particularly hot and humid day painting the outside of a house. Our crew of 6 people were sweating profusely and drinking Gatorade in the shade to keep from fainting and falling off the ladders. It was really miserable weather. I was being compassionate and allowing for whatever breaks were necessary to keep body and soul together. This young priest about 32 years old got so tired and disgusted with the day that he decided to quit and walk off the job. I know it's shameful to have an inexperienced priest act like that. But he told me he was too old for this stuff (he used a different word) and I couldn't help laughing. I was first shocked at his behavior and the part of him that had to make an effort that was apparently very undisciplined. But more than that I was struck by how young he was and how his words did not match that observation. He said, "I am too old for this blank." That made me laugh because I was at least ten years older and I was out there suffering the heat of the day just like the rest of the crew. It is amazing what kind of thoughts fill our minds when we are a little stressed out or challenged in some way. We just go to a place that is completely lacking in faith and selfish because we want to go there. He did walk off the job and pretty soon he walked out of his calling to the priesthood. He hasn't functioned since. He wanted it his way and he sure got it. I am not saying that if a person was medically losing it, he shouldn't have gone home. But he was perfectly fine; he just didn't want to do what he didn't want to do.

So count the cost of your wanting things your way. You have every right to have them. But do you want what the consequences are of those decisions? Can you live with closing the door on the possibility of your life with God, Jesus and Mary just because of a moment's gratification or sensual satisfaction? Can you handle the cost of such a decision? I couldn't.

The Gospel as Revealed to Me, Vol. 7, p. 207
"Do not allow yourselves to be harmed by the following proud thoughts: "I am strong and the evil of other people will not affect me. I am just, and even if I listen to unjust people, I

remain just." Man is a deep abyss in which all the elements of good and evil can be found. The former, the help of God, assists us in improving and becoming kings and queens; the latter, the evil passions and bad friendship, help us to grow more wicked and to reign noxiously. All the germs of evil and all the longing for good are latent in man by God's loving will, and by the wicked will of Satan, who influences, tempts, and instigates, whereas God attracts, comforts and loves. Satan tries to seduce, he works to conquer God. And God does not always win, because creatures are heavy until they choose love as their law, and being heavy they debase themselves and crave more easily for anything that is immediate satisfaction and gratification of the lowest instincts of man."

"From what I am telling you about human weakness, you can understand how necessary it is not to trust yourselves and to watch your neighbor very carefully, lest you should join the poison of an impure conscience to that already fermenting in you. When you understand that a friend is the ruin of hearts, when his words upset your consciences, when his advice is the cause of scandal, you must forsake the harmful friendship. If you persist you would end by seeing your soul perish, because you would pass on to actions that remove from God and prevent a hardened conscience from understanding God's inspirations. If everyone guilty of grave sins could or wanted to speak explaining how they came to commit such sins, one would see that there is always a bad friendship at the origin."

"Do not trust those who after fighting you without any reason, load you with honors and gifts. Do not trust those who praise every action of yours and who praise everybody and everything: they commend loungers as being hard workers, adulterers as faithful spouses, thieves as honest people, violent people as being meek, liars as being sincere, wicked people as being loyal and they point out the worst disciples as exemplary ones. They do so to ruin you and to make use of your downfall for their artful aims. Shun those who want to intoxicate you with praises and promises to *make you do things that you would refuse to do if you were not intoxicated. And when you have sworn loyalty to someone, have nothing to do with their enemies. They would approach you only to harm the one who they hate and do so through your very help. Keep your eyes open. I said: Be as wise as serpents besides being as simple as doves. Because simplicity is holy when dealing with spiritual matters, but to live in the world without damaging oneself and one's friends, it is necessary to possess the cunning that is capable of finding out the artfulness of those who hate saints. The world is a nest of snakes. You must become acquainted with the world and its systems. And then, staying like doves not in the mire where serpents are, but in the shelter of a high cliff, have the simple hearts of the children of God. And pray and pray because I solemnly tell you that the Great Serpent is hissing around you, and you are therefore in great danger and those who are not vigilant will perish. Yes, among the disciples there are some who will perish with great joy of Satan and infinite grief of the Christ..... Be vigilant my friends. Watch over yourselves and other people, take heed of what other people say to you and of what your consciences tell you. And if you cannot see clearly by yourselves, come to me, for I am the Light."*

You were given freedom when God conceived you. Use that freedom wisely. All the things that you choose will be given to you. Be careful that you really want them and the consequences they create. If you need help deciding, you might want a real relationship with a teacher who can guide you into the safe pastures of your own divinity. The teacher has chosen already and is one with the Father and will not lead you astray. When you can admit your need of help, the teacher is given to you.

ALLOWING YOURSELF TO BE HEALED

All healing comes from God. It is God who animates and vitalizes every part of creation. So God vitalizes human beings. The life you carry and express is God's life moving in you. When you have run yourself down and tired yourself out emotionally, mentally and physically, you are in need of recharging. When you persistently run down your energies by misuse of emotions and thinking, you deplete your spiritual energies to such an extent that symptoms could result. Symptoms only occur when your thinking and feeling have gotten persistent enough to cause the physical to manifest your prayer of action. Whatever you consistently put out in mind or emotions will cause an effect after a period of time. The body is the last thing to respond to a persistent misconception. Your thoughts and feelings may be in accord with God or they might be out of phase with how God thinks and feels. If your energies are out of phase with God, what we call "out of accord" then you are using your energies contrary to the way God created things. It is only a matter of time before your body symptomatizes and manifests some kind of illness.

If you think illnesses just happen to people, you are not looking very deeply at how creation works and how God works. God satisfies the desire of every living thing. So God makes sure you have what we want. If you put out a particular energy, you will get that energy back. The Law of Cause and Effect works inexorably. Jesus treated the cause of illnesses. When Jesus came across a man lying on a stretcher unable to walk, he said, "Arise!" Jesus commanded him and the man stood up fully healed. It is that simple. If you have that knowing, it will work. If you aren't sure, then it won't work, because you are still thinking it won't work. If you go to the cause, you can heal like Jesus did. If a person

17

is ill and you find the cause by finding out why they have that illness, then you don't have to try. You will find out and then you treat the cause. You don't treat the illness. But you have to get really simple in order to heal or it won't work.

A realpriest does not merely work on the material plane. They have to work on the spiritual plane where the cause is. They see the actual physical symptoms, but do not get caught up in those. They do not give them any life by imagining that they are real. The symptoms are merely demonstrations of the effect of your thinking and feeling that you may not even be aware of. You don't have to go around shouting words of healing in order to heal someone. You have to have your mind straight so that your thinking is clear. It takes a strong, powerful mind and pure spirituality in order to truly heal. You have to be able to see the image of evil and unreality in order to know it isn't true and not be affected by it. You have to know it is not true and at the same time you have to know the inner divinity of the person you are treating.

Prayer is really anything you think or say. Because every thought is something that will carry energy into God and God will respond to those words and thoughts manifesting them for you. Healing is no different. You can lay your hands on someone and let the power of God and the Holy Spirit move through you to heal them. Or you can have a conviction that the person will be healed and go on your way because you know it is done. You use the Law the same in both cases. In a deeper way, you have to heal yourself of the idea that someone is ill. Then the healing will conform to what you say, do and think. They will get well because you see and declare the perfection of that person in spite of what they are thinking to cause the imbalance in the first place. When the woman touched the hem of the Master's garment, Jesus didn't say anything, and yet she was healed. It was because of his consciousness of healing, His radiation of love and giving from his soul and body that the healing took place. If you keep your mind straight, you will be able to do the same. That is the beauty of healing.

People don't want explanations when it comes to healing. They want results, so forget trying to convince them of the possibility of God and of God's power to heal. You have to know that God heals and know that it works.

People talk about magnetic healing using the energy that comes through the body or through the hands. When people touch as in therapeutic touch or healing touch, this is magnetic energy moving from one body into another. The practitioner does not have to have any knowledge of God to do it. They're not praying at all, just rubbing or touching your body. Magnetic healing draws out the disease while spiritual healing puts the power of God and the Christ force into a person to remove the disease. A magnetic healer might get good results if they know that what they were doing works and would get better results if they prayed and knew God. Sometimes the magnetic healers do not know how to discharge the negative energy or other things that come out of the person they are treating. They will pick up negative things from the person and carry that around with them for a while. Your hands on various parts of the body will release tension and relax pressure in that area. Even in walking you stimulate all the organs of the body through the nerve endings in the bottom of the feet. Each organ has a relationship to the eight planets in our Solar System. Everything is related in our system.

Jesus used his knowing and his Word to project this power. Jesus said, "Of all these things that I do, so shall you do and even greater than these." Anything you make up your mind to accept will become a reality for you. A person who is hypochondriacal will imagine they have all kinds of illnesses and will take medicines as a crutch. They feel lonely without their medications. It has become such a habit for them that they just can't get along without them.

19

Physicians have known for years that it is all in your head and they know that when you decide to have something, real or imagined, you will manifest those symptoms. Doctors used to give colored pills as placebos and patients would experience definite relief of symptoms. Everyone has the same God-given power to create whatever you want. We are all the same in that way except our soul experience and personality are different because of past life experience. Most people are still looking at life through past-life lenses and that is what keeps you down.

It would be a little strange to see someone in need and walk right up to them and lay your hands on them and give them a blessing. So if that is not possible or comfortable for you or them, just ask God to release the life force in that person and see the person becoming filled with life and movement. This is a blessing that you can give whether they know it is happening or not. That person is God's creation and so you can definitely give them some of God's vital life. If they are supposed to be healed by it then they will be healed. If you think it is your imagination, you are partially right. You would say you looked and saw or you were trying to see the light within them. If you couldn't, you would need to relax some more and close your eyes and look, and then you will see. Just look and you will see if you want to see. Do it and don't talk about it or you will lose the constancy of the power that is being built up inside of you. The ones who know how to do this don't talk about it much because they are becoming walking sources of healing just by their presence around other people.

The spiritual body is perfect. In a disease the energy of the physical illness has lowered the energy of the spiritual body to such an extent that a symptom or illness occurs. Foreign pathology might not manifest in a disease but just be present as a weakness in the body. But sometimes it takes on a form of a growth or cancer of some sort. It might get to the place where an entity starts to be created but usually it is a chemical condition foreign to the body. The disease originates in the physical body because there is not sufficient strength in the spiritual body to maintain health. When you pray, you are bringing back the potential of the spiritual body and recharging it so it is strong again. Immediately a healing takes place in the physical. The intelligence of God, through your God Self and soul direct and guide the power of God to move in and remove the dross from the physical and bring about a healing. The poisons and pathology that were allowed to accumulate in particular parts of the body are removed in the blessing.

Because the spiritual body is perfect, something else must have caused the disease or illness. A person's willful living is what caused it. You can see the disease in manifested form, but that does not make it real. Yes, there is actual suffering from the situation, but you have to know, if you are treating a person, that the spiritual body of this person is perfect. The cause of the illness is some unreal thing the person has accepted in their mind. Are you going to heal them or aren't you? They control their universe and they have free will and free choice to hold onto whatever they want to hold onto. You can't violate their freedom and interfere unless they have asked you for help. If they do not want any help, we leave them in their illness because they want it that way. If they want help, then we are ready to help change their world. They may be a little upset at what a perfect universe feels like afterward, but we merely did what they asked us to do.

We are not looking for or accepting evil. That is what people create for themselves and they may be enjoying that for the present. You have to let people know that you are able to help and see what they want after that. Sometimes you can come right out directly and ask, "Why don't you want to be well?" They sometimes get angry but maybe they'll come around and ask for help later. We need to warn you, people will not love you because you heal them. They will be disturbed mostly that you know more about them than they do and most people hate the idea of anyone knowing more than they do. People have a right to make their territory any way they want it and they do. In healing a person the change takes place immediately but the body might have to slough off the negative energy that it is carrying.

Sickness is nothing but sin and it can be healed and relieved if you deliver enough power there. If the person wants to be healed, they will. If they don't, there is nothing you can do about it. The illness has an electrical odor that is given off and you will be able to smell it when the healing takes place because the radiation of the negative energy will be discharged when the healing takes place and move into the room where the blessing was done. If you become conscious of the spiritual body, then you will be effective in your treatments. You will be using the Light of Christ and moving that energy into people to recharge their spiritual bodies.

Vol. 4, p. 115
"And passing from things to people, there is no event, no tear, no joy, no birth, no death, no sterility and prolific maternity, no long marriage life or early widowhood, no misfortune of calamities and diseases, or prosperity of wealth and health, which does not have its good reason for being, even if it does not appear as such to the short-sightedness and pride of men, who see and judge through the cataracts and fogs typical of imperfect things. But the Eye of God, the Infinite Thought of God, sees and knows. The secret of living free from sterile doubts, which irritate, exhaust and poison the days on earth, is to believe that God does everything for a good intelligent reason that God does what God does for love, not for the stolid intention of tormenting for the sake of tormenting. God had created the angels. And some of them, who did not want to believe that the level of glory at which they had been placed was good, rebelled and with their minds parched by

lack of faith in their Lord, they attempted to assail the unreachable throne of God. They opposed their discordant unjust pessimistic thoughts to the harmonious reasons of the faithful angels, and pessimism, which is lack of faith, changed them from spirits of light into spirits of darkness."

Vol. 2, p. 302

"Jesus means Savior. There is a salvation of the soul and a salvation of the body. Who pronounces the Name of Jesus with true faith is freed from disease and sin, because in every spiritual or physical disease there is the claw of Satan who creates physical diseases to drive people to rebellion and desperation through the pains of the flesh, and he creates moral or spiritual diseases to lead souls to damnation. ... Through him disease and death entered the world. And crime and corruption also entered the world through him. When you see anyone tortured by misfortune, you can be sure that he suffers on account of Satan. When you see one who is the cause of misfortune, you may conclude that he is an instrument of Satan.

"Illness is a disorder in the order. But used by Satan in the order given by God, has brought with it the illness of the flesh and its consequences, that is, death or sorrowful heredity. Man inherited from Adam and Eve the original sin. But not only that. And the stain has expanded wider and wider embracing the three branches of man: the flesh more and more vicious and consequently weak and diseased, the morals prouder and prouder and thus corrupted, the spirit more and more skeptical and thus more and more idolatrous. That is why it is necessary, as I did with the poor half-wit, to teach the Name that puts Satan to flight, engraving It on minds and hearts, placing It on one's ego as a seal of ownership."

HEALER OR AGITANT

Either you are a force for healing or you are an agitant. Your energy can be smooth and flowing or it can be jarring and disjointed. You are putting out vibrations and energy all the time. What is the quality of the energy you are putting out? Is it peaceful? Is it tranquil? Is it joyous and uplifting? Is it depressed and sullen? Are you are depressed and unhappy person? I have news for you. The spiritual path is not for the depressed or angry. If you are depressed or angry, you are still healing and have not put your foot on the spiritual path as yet. There are certain things that have to be cleaned up and removed before you could honestly say you were following a path. I know that sounds hard and tough, but it is the truth. We find it necessary to clean people up quite a lot before they are even teachable. In many cases, there are so many idiosyncratic anomalies in the average person's character that a great deal of cleaning and removing is required in or for the person to be able to hear what we are teaching them.

You can't help Jesus and Mary and God, if you are not of the same mind as they are. If you don't know their mind and the way they see things, then you can't be part of the supervisory team of priests. I know many of you do not feel called to that illustrious office and maybe do not wish to function that way in this lifetime. That is fine. You can still be part of a wonderful spiritual community. As disciples of Jesus and Mary, you have a chance to become who you really are as a soul. You have a way placed in front of you whereby you can be an Illumined being, radiant with the Christ Light. You have the opportunity to become one with God regardless of the work that your soul is called to do. But one thing I want to get extremely clear in your mind and that is that you need to follow God and not your own

25

opinions and dislikes. I hear people say they don't' like this and they don't see themselves doing that. How many times has that same person actually submitted those opinions to God for some real perspective? Not very often. Because if they did, they would get the surprise of a lifetime. They might be informed about having served in the priesthood in another life. They might be shown their failure in trying to serve God in the past and they would understand that they were anxious about making the same mistake again. It could be any of a number of things, but the truth through it all would be that they were trying to do it themselves and disregard God's input. That is a serious mistake born of fear and pride. You are not aware of all the reasons why things happen, are you? You can't see that far ahead to why something needs to be done now, do you? So how is it that you are the expert on what is best for you, when you have God inside you trying to tell you what would be best for you? It is a little silly to try to figure anything out at all, because God knows what will make sense.

Are you radiating light, peace and joy? Or are you waiting for something to happen? If you are waiting for something to happen, you are still acting like a passive recipient of whatever the parents dish out to you. There is nothing passive about shining the light or deciding to let love move through you. There is nothing passive about deciding to connect with God and form a relationship with God in a personal way. The main reason why people don't want to believe in God as a real being that you can relate to is because it makes it real. If something is real, it becomes a thing you would die for.

Do you feel peaceful most of the time? Have you known profound peace or has it been like feeling tired? Profound peace is having no fear or worries because all is taken care of in your soul. You feel the connection to God's love and know that God is there to help when you ask which makes everything simple. When you get complicated in your mind, you are actually making excuses for action or for letting things go. When you fear, you are lacking in peace. Peace is the most important signature of God. By this sign, Jesus would ask that God's peace be in the house where he was staying or visiting. He brought this peace with him wherever he walked so that people would feel relaxed about letting God love them. Peace is the main feature of a disciple that is in the process of transformation and is experiencing God's love. The only reason a person would not be experiencing God's love is that they were willfully staying away from God. They would have separated themselves from connection to God in a number of ways. When you fear, you reject love. When you get angry, you are holding a grudge or a resentment which is filled with indignation and pride. God withdraws from the proud. Fear, pride, resentment, anger, jealousy, avarice, lust and gluttony all separate you from the peace and love of God. Those are considered deadly sins, because the death they cause is your separation from God. Flee those negative things and you will be able to experience the peace of God. God wants people to be with God and feel that profound peace that is God's nature.

If you carry that peace, you are a living example of Jesus and Mary who are the Masters of peace. You will reflect them in all of your thoughts, feelings and actions. Then you will be a force of healing and people around you will feel the connection you have and will want to let go of the troubles and anger they are carrying and holding. Letting those negative feelings go will be the direction of growth for all you influence. If people want to keep their negative energy, then they will quickly move away from you and it will be increasingly clear to you who wants God and who doesn't. Most people will choose to not have the love of God. Jesus said at least two thirds of the people will choose the darkness and refuse the Light of God in these last days. Don't be surprised at this. Jesus forewarned us that things would turn out this way. Just be faithful and don't worry about who chooses what. Two people will be grinding at a mill, one will be taken and the other left. Two will be working in the field, one will be taken and the other left. Jesus prophesied about this 2000 years ago.

What heals people? What is the most important part of healing? Whenever Jesus healed someone, he said their sins were forgiven. He also told them to go and sin no more. That was a consistent message. Jesus said you must repent of your errors, sins and negative energy in order to be forgiven. You cannot be forgiven if you hold those feelings inside and continue to indulge them. You must forgive or God cannot forgive you. Many of you have been having the experience of completely forgiving everyone from your past of the things you were holding resentment and anger about. You were not even aware in many cases of how much anger, resentment and hurt you were holding. It has been extremely important for your whole spiritual life to be able to be a successful disciple. You cannot move into the relationship with God unless and until you have let go of the holdings and attachment that you have to people who you expected things from. I know this is old news. I know you think you are done with your past. But I have news for you, whenever you are angry; you are still caught in your past. You are still working out your anger to significant people in your past that you are presently taking out on the ones closest to you. Lack of peace is proof that you are still holding on to hurts and resentments from early in life. You have not forgiven. Most of you say you will forgive if those people would just be sorry and apologize for what they have done. Jesus did not say you can only forgive if the other person is sorry. Forgive means you give before they do. You give first. You don't wait for them to pay you back before you forgive them. If they repair the damage, then you don't have to forgive them, because they already paid it back. Forgiveness would be unnecessary if everyone made amends. You would just let go and relax when they paid you back. But forgiveness is important to do before, while you are holding on to the resentment.

LIFE IN GOD

The more you devote your life to God, the more God takes care of you. Do not worry about anything. When you sit on the fence between two worlds, you will be torn by opposing desires and motivations. You want the life in God, the love and the blessings. You want the things most others have in the world. You feel drawn into the silence and stillness of meditation and yet you want the excitement and exhilaration of what everyone wants – money, sex and power. You want to be known and seen; you want to have powerful influence on others, you want to control things and people and you want to make things happen the way you want them to happen. You want to make a big splash so people can know what you do not feel – that you are important, loved and good. You would not want those things outside you if you thought you were good and fine with the love you are experiencing.

When you are completely still and receptive, you start to feel the love and the peace that your mind cannot understand. The mind must simply relax and be awed by the presence of God. If you want to be free from stress and confusion, allow this stillness to settle into your body and mind as you open to being completely nothing.

Let's Meditate Now.

Be nothing so that God can be everything in you. Be totally receptive and let the flashes of God's intelligence stream across your awareness. Open your mind and heart and let the grace come in to change every part of you. Be putty in God's hands. Be an ocean wave pulsed through creation by the mind of God and roll with it. You are not in charge. You do not control anything at all. Accept your status as created.

You are the created, not the Creator. Meditate on the fact that you were thought up in the mind of God and breathed out into the world as an expression of the one true God. You have no other purpose. You are not alone even though a thousand voices scream at you. The voices of the demons yell in your face that you are not enough, that you are too small and weak to amount to anything. Plug up your ears to those disastrous voices. Chant your acceptance of God in the face of those inharmonious voices from the deep. Be one of the brave souls who defy negation and cling to the bright light of truth.

There is no peace in the world. There is no light in the world unless you carry light to the world. Your connection will be the light that others can notice and rely on. They will see your light in the distance and be drawn like moths towards it, unable to resist it. Shine brightly for the souls that yearn for God, for goodness. Be simple and do not boast of your light, or imagine your light can be embellished or made magnificent. You can simply be what your Father created you to be – a light shining in the darkness. What quality, what brightness with which you shine is not up to you, it is up to God. How that light attracts souls is also not up to you, it is designed by God. The reflection of the one light passing through the prism of you, with all your faults and foibles, makes you shine in a particular way that God blesses. Others are drawn by God's decree to your light and that is the only way souls come to God. You do nothing of yourself in drawing them. Jesus said, "No one comes to the Father except the Father draws them." So you do not have anything to do with it, except that you were willing to be used to meet them when God puts them in your way. Then love them like your own son or daughter. Make their first contact with a disciple be so sweet and radiant that they never forget that first meeting with one who follows God.

All moments of meditation and prayer should be seen as time with God, intimate and personal relating with God. If you approach these times as meaningful and personal, you will prepare yourself, much like you would tidy up your house, wash your face, comb your hair and make yourself presentable to one that you want to be close to. You would not be casual or take the relationship for granted. You would value the time together and appreciate all of the moments and energies of the relating. You are building a muscle of relationship with God. Come to God honestly and trusting, knowing that you will be taken care of in the embrace. God is the most pure love and all you can ever hope for in relationship. God longs for this connecting and will support you completely. You must come free from wanting to control or otherwise work God. God will not make deals with any of the creation. God will not be mocked at your attempts to put one over on God. You cannot lie to God without God withdrawing from you a little. You have to come clean and open your heart without protection, pride or fear. When God feels pride in you, God will back away and make you get rid of that. If you come to God empty of anything you can be proud of or without attributes you think might impress, then God comes in the fullness of God's love and power to bless you.

Even if you hold things back from God, God will notice and you will not have the fullness of relationship that you planned. God sees the little pockets of holding onto a dream, onto a woman or a man, onto a fleeting moment of fame or expression of power, and those places will prevent God from entering deeply into relationship with you. Those dreams and fantasies that you hold onto, show that you have a large god in the place of God. You have kept your dream to yourself because you could not trust anyone with that special of an ideal. God is not allowed there because your pride controls it completely. You are holding on and holding out for a greater god than the one true God. Because of that, God cannot come to you and bless you because you held some part of you separate. That is pride. You feel that only you can keep that dream safe. Only you can value that part of your dream and you did not ask God about it because you did not want any interference. God might disturb your idea of what might fulfill you and make you happy. When you control things like that, then God is ousted and will not be able to help you. You have to empty even those pipedreams in order to be truly humble before God. Get simple and let them go, trusting that God will take care of you. When you are willful like that and have to manage every dream on your own, where is God - left out and so are you.

There is no joy without God. There is no real life without God. An idea of God is lifeless and meaningless. It has to be a matter of your heart and an actual relationship or it will not satisfy. The people who think allot about God may never really attain the experience of relating to God as a real being, a perfect love. They will hold God in a certain cerebral container in their head that they manage and show off their knowledge about. They would have to use God's language and description of God in order to communicate God to others. But they are proud and demean God shrinking God down to a size that resembles a small concept in a corner of their created brain. That is demeaning and disrespectful. If they knew God, they would be on their knees. They would be humbled by the sheer power of God's love and it would short out their little brain in a flash. God moves that quickly to receptive souls. Try it sometime.

DISTURBANCES AS A GOAD TO YOUR SPIRITUAL DEVELOPMENT

Life dishes up surprises for us every day. It is a rare day that something doesn't happen that challenges you or startles you a little bit. People do things that we did not anticipate; circumstances arise that are unplanned and make us adapt to them; and people do and say things we cannot foresee. If you don't like surprises here on earth, you will probably be miserable. Things happen and you are often not consulted about them. People are not predictable and you can't know ahead of time how they will respond to situations.

You have all had the experience of planning out your day to a tee and visualizing smooth sailing of events throughout and then something happens to mess up the plan. It is a blessed day when nothing unexpected or unplanned arises to throw a wrench in the works. A day that just flows smoothly from one event or task to another without a hitch is exceptional and magical. How you handle the surprises makes a huge difference and determines whether you are going to mature spiritually or not. If you react to every change of plans or each turn in the road with anger, hurt or fear, then you demonstrate a very tenuous spirituality. You show your immaturity to handle the fortunes and misfortunes of life. If you get scared each time something is out of the ordinary or outside your concept of how things should unfold, then you are fragile inside and still very hurt by your past. Your fears give you away and they show that you are still traumatized by your history. Maybe it is his story or her story, but it is your history. If you are still living out your past wounds, you are not grown up yet and still living in the past ducking each blow or insult when you were a child. If you are still feeling the feelings of childhood, you have not grown up yet and are still under the dominion of your care-givers. Separating from them and healing is the work you are faced with if that is the case.

How you handle changes in plans or jostling by other people shows your inner strength and connection to your soul. A person who is connected to their soul is not fazed by the words or decisions of other people, because they know themselves and are not disturbed by anything outside themselves. People can make whatever decisions they need to make and it has nothing to do with you. People can also try to hurt you and it won't hurt you because you are connected to the love inside and that cannot be dislodged by anything people say or do. If you are not looking out for what people might say or think about you, then you won't care what their opinions might be about you. If you know yourself, then what does it matter what others think, do or say?

There are two kinds of disturbances that you can experience: from outside of your soul and from inside your soul. These two might be called from darkness or from God. Yes, God can disturb you and stretch you to love more or be more for others than you have been expressing. God can jostle you and disturb your sensibilities especially if you have a rigid mindset of what is appropriate and what is not. If you are stiff about rules and regulations, then, out of love for you, God might see how constricting that is for your soul and help you dissolve that pattern. God might put you in situations where you are forced to see things from another person's point of view. God might put you in someone else's shoes and have you walk a mile in them to feel what another human being might be experiencing. This will be a healing and a blessing for you since you were previously so convinced that the way you were looking at things was so correct, so right. God might want more Spirit to flow through you and your thinking might be too tight for the amount of love and light God wants to shove through you. When you relax, it will flow. God's disturbances should be a welcome mist of love flowing your way. You should acknowledge this with gratitude and appreciation and not fear it or be angry at God for giving you this attention. God wants what is best for you and everyone around you and so will, at times, mess up your patterns so that you can be more useful to God. You should pray for this and welcome it when it comes. It is a blessing. It might burn you a little and purge you of the negative feelings, behaviors and attitude that prevent you from serving, loving and giving as you are capable. It might be a purging that has to drive the darkness from you in answer to your prayer that you become prepared to serve God. God will get your former little self out of the way for the greater Self to express through you. You can't do this yourself, so you are not in control of the process once you have asked for help. Let go and let God do it.

The negative disturbances are always of the darkness, always evil. You can be disturbed by fears suggested to you that you are unsafe. This fear is designed to sell you on the idea that you should have control of everything that happens and if you don't, then life is being unfair and unsafe. This is a complete lie. This is God's life, not yours and you are given everything you need to manage your life in accord with God's will. You are capable of whatever life dishes out to you. God knows you can do anything and has given you the power to do that. God is inside of you and has the power to overcome or master any challenge or overcome any obstacle. If you try to do it yourself, as the darkness suggests in its subtle version of suggesting you should be in control of everything that comes and everything that happens, you will fail. The darkness will then tell you that you relied on God and that is why it failed. But it was your fear and believing the lies of the demons that made you fail. You froze up when you should trust God, just the opposite of what God was trying to teach you.

Anything that causes disturbance or disorder is evil. It is instigated by demons and is under the watchful notice of the satanic being. Disorder and hatred of God are the complete and only motive for Satan. If the darkness can get you to be scared, it wins. If it can get you to doubt, worry and be anxious, it wins. If it can get you to be paranoid that people are out to get you, it wins. Ultimately, the darkness wants you so scared, angry and prideful that you go into despair and hopelessness and just give up. When you get close to despair you won't care what happens or what you do and you will stop running your own ship. In this state of you giving up, the demons can dance on your head and influence you to do whatever they want. What do they want really? They want to take a human being, a divine son or daughter of God, and make them a monkey that is controlled by lust, fear, power and pride. They want to do this because it mocks the Father. It laughs at God's most beautiful creation – human beings. It hates God and everything God loves. Why? Because they are stupid and nasty. They are hate, as God is love. They enjoy disturbing human beings, they gloat when a servant of God falls from their mission because they are victors over that soul that gave themselves up to selfishness, lust, pride or power. It is so sad that people fall for these tactics and yet most people allow themselves to be disturbed by them.

If you are disturbed by feeling slighted by other people, overlooked for promotion, under-appreciated for your abilities, unacknowledged for your gifts, you are under the influence of pride. Pride comes before the Fall. You will fall if you puff yourself up and demand acknowledgement from others for your gifts. They actually are not your gifts because God owns all gifts, talents and virtues. Those virtues, talents and abilities can only be loaned to you from God and they are not yours. All inventions and inspirations were God's before they were dispensed to the planets and to the beings that live on them. We are recipients of God's blessings and we don't own anything. Any disorder in the

38

order of the universe is instigated by the dark forces. We are not afraid of them. We are not fazed by their efforts to control us or influence us. We look at them and reduce them to ashes by our glance. They are dust in the wind and nothing to us who have completely committed to God. We have chosen God always and so these influences fall like dust against our edifice of faith. We are your examples of how to handle the disturbance and disorder of the darkness. Do not pay any attention to it and it will not get a foothold inside you. Flee all fear, impatience, anxiety and pride. Do not indulge yourself sensually to give no root to the darkness within you. Be pure in heart and obedient to the reality of love.

The other analysis that you should make in practice is whether a disturbance comes from the outside, or from within. If the disturbance comes from within, you might be purging out an old pattern and it has come up for review and release. If that is the case, then God is causing it to purge and is lifting by God's grace this troublesome pattern out of you. That is a blessing and God's love for you that does that. The other disturbance we have already talked about from within is when God unsettles you and stirs you up to help you change and be more of what you can be for God. Then you are becoming more useful and of clearer service as the old is being washed out of you. If the disturbance is from without, then it is of the darkness trying to make you scared of something outside. The disturbance might be to pull you out of your soul and make you think you are just a bundle of appetites and emotions that should be placated or fulfilled. This is sensuality and pride. You should be entitled to a break, to some creature comforts and this will repay you for the hardships you have suffered and been exposed to. You deserve a break today and you should indulge yourself immediately as it is only right that you should not have to have it so hard. That appealed to your pride and the conclusion that people treated you badly and that is was not fair. But how your parents treated you was fair and you deserved that because you treated people that way in another lifetime. You should have forgiven them after you got into the teen years and let go of it. But you have been trying to recoup the loss and redress the wound to make up for how horrible it was. But if it was deserved, then you should just call it even and move on with a humble heart and a dedicated resolve to be different in the future. Why don't you resolve that today and let go of your need to be entitled or coddled because of your past pain. That pain was not given by God, it was created by you. So get over yourself and move into perfection and serving.

From now on, embrace disturbances as a challenge to overcome your tendency to fall into darkness or as a way to embrace the stretching and growing that God wants for you. For once in your life, try to stop orchestrating your growth and progress and let God and your teachers lead you out of your shallow life into the life of grace and the life of love.

BECOMING A LEADER

Have you ever visualized yourself as a leader? Can you see yourself being the example of what others should do? Do you have what it takes to be the one who is followed by other people? Are you comfortable having people do what you do and say what you say and move like you move? Do you know that that is exactly what a real disciple of Jesus and Mary becomes?

A real disciple is one who has taken on the life where virtue and integrity are more important than pleasing other people or tiptoeing daintily through life. If you don't want to be noticed, then don't be a real disciple. If you don't want to stand out, then don't wear the colors and carry the energy of a disciple. If you are virtuous, you will be unusual on this planet. If you have integrity, you will be one of the few. If you are in the minority, like any real disciple is, then you will stand out. If you stand out, people will notice you and be happy with you and inspired, or they will be offended and try to hurt you. If what you express to other people is respect for life, respect for God and our planet, then you will be unique and different. Respecting life is not just appreciating some trees and shrubs. Respecting our planet does not involve the superficial dismay over an oil spill or large floating masses of plastic in our oceans. Those concerns are good, but any 3rd grader can have such care and sadness over these things. Respecting God means you love and appreciate all the substances and energies that God supports. You will love and support whatever God loves and supports, which is practically everything in creation except darkness and meanness. God supports life and human beings. God does not support meanness, lust, pornography, self-indulgence, hatred, anger, pride or fear. So if you are a real disciple, you flee from every one of those

41

things. You resolve not to be like that and you delete those behaviors and desires from your repertoire forever.

You see how rare a real disciple is? A person with integrity who does not stoop to negative behavior or bad moods is unusual in this world. If you are like this, you will be one in a hundred thousand. If you know people, you have to understand that everyone notices when someone is a little different or who marches to a different beat than the rest of the people. You stand out because you represent Christ. You are noticeable because you stand for love, respect for God and virtuous integrity. When you stand out like this, you will be leading. It is inevitable. It is necessary. Someone has to lead in any social grouping. It is inconceivable that in a group of people that every person is at the same place emotionally or spiritually. It would be phenomenal if everyone understood and appreciated the reality of life in the same way at the same time. But that is not the case. It probably never will be the case. Even when all the humans on the earth are Illumined, there will still need to be priest/leaders who will demonstrate and lead people to the next level of development.

We have seen in a group of women that when one woman knows what should be done, she will often get mad at the other women for not carrying their weight. What she is really saying is that she wants the other women to understand what she understands and to carry the responsibility equally with her for the simple reason that she does not want to lead. She wants everyone to do things together so they can all be one. We can all do it together. But that is unrealistic. Someone always knows more, sees more or understands more than someone else and that person is the designated leader in that situation – simply because they have the super-vision. Why is it that women do not want to lead? What kind of insidious subservience is operating that a woman won't stand up and just lead when she sees what apparently the others around her don't? The group mind says, "Can't we all get along and do it together equally?" The reason this does not work is because everyone is in a different place and consciousness and are not ready to take on the responsibility in the same way. One person sees earlier or deeper than someone else. It is the way of life. Another person just does not have the whole picture and cannot feel the urgency of what is important in a situation because they are not prepared to see it yet. Someone has to lead. We could say it more politely that someone is leading by virtue of a deeper understanding or knowing or vision. If you see more or know more, then you are leading others.

Try not to feel bad about this. It is the pattern in families that parents are ahead of the children as the instructors of the children. The parents are the protectors and the way showers for the children. God inspires people among their peers to see more or feel more than the others and that person is the designated leader of the others in that area of life. Spiritually, it is the same. One person looks into the spiritual world and experiences more of God than another because they opened for that. One feels a greater abundance of love and closeness to God because they opened for that and prepared for it by meditation or devotion. Another chooses to learn helpful behaviors and compassionate concern for others in order to know how things work and how to help other people in becoming what they want. A leader rises up in the midst of other people by a desire to give, serve, love, shine. Others take notice and have their feelings about that. People can be jealous, hopeless, hurt, angry, fearful, or hateful. In a positive light, people can be thankful someone is leading, appreciative, respectful and grateful.

A leader leads. A leader sees ahead and is one step ahead of the rest. It is not a race, but they have the sight to see what needs to be done and they get it before the others do. A leader speaks up and says things to the rest of the people about what they care about and what has been shown to them. Their enthusiasm and life force inspires the others to move along in the direction the leader envisions. A leader is one who takes responsibility for the others and carries them when they are too weak or sluggish to move along with their own energy. The world needs leaders. Jesus trained leaders in the Apostles and asked them to lead when he ascended. Each disciple is being asked to lead in the same way. If your discipleship is real, then you are making great strides in changing from the old person to the new person. Your faults are dissolving and your bad habits are dying. Your sight is opening and your abilities to love and give are growing. In a short time, you will have risen above those who are still sleeping and have not shaken off the darkness.

If you are leading, then you will be loved or hated. Get used to it and accept it. Like the wise sages say, "Think of praise or blame as one." When it is cloudy, people will complain about you and say bad things. When it is sunny, people will celebrate with you and praise you. Neither praise nor blame is lasting or meaningful in the great scheme of things. If God praises you, then you should be happy and take note. If God chastises you, then take notice, thank God and fix yourself. God's evaluations of you are the only thing you should be paying attention to anyway. Pleasing God and expressing God is the only motivator for a real disciple. God is above all interests and concerns for a disciple who loves God with their whole mind, heart, soul and strength.

Holding consciousness is the action of carrying spiritual reality and knowing. It means you have integrity, that you are one person throughout your whole being. You have no disjointed parts. You are not divided within yourself or fighting with yourself. Integrity means whole, that you are wholly you. You won't be surprised that something is inside of you warring with your soul or your heart and mind because it won't be happening. All of you is on board with one vision and one purpose. That is rare on the earth at present and very few people have such a simple life. It is simple when there is no war going on inside you. It is simple when all of you is completely for what you value and what you care about. It is simple when you are a real disciple of Jesus and Mary because you devote all your life energies, thought and feelings to the mission that they carry for this planet and its peoples. A real disciple is a powerful being who moves the mountains of earth. People are definitely going to notice you. You will be shining with a confidence in God that is unmovable and unshakable. Do you know such people? Are your brothers and sisters like that? Are you becoming one of those?

We want all of our members to lead a life that is an example to other people. That constitutes leadership. We want the sisters and brothers to be leading the way showing people how to serve and give of themselves without thought of themselves. We want our students to be an example to others of obedience to their teacher, obedience and love for God above all else and not distracted by the allurements of the world. We eventually want everyone in our order to be leading other people. But you have to be in relationship with God to do that. You have to be fully on board with our mission to demonstrate that vision to others by your example. We are dedicated to wake up the world. We are determined to make a difference in people's lives. We are fired up to change the world and we expect our leadership to be noticed. We are leading you into the eternal life.

If you follow well, you whole life will be healed and your patterns will be changed from what you experienced before. You will raise up and be new as a soul and an expression of God. That constitutes leader, because only a small percent of the population will have undergone such training and discipline. You will be leader if you take our lessons.

A WHOLE LOT OF LOVE

It is going to take a lot of love to get you to the place where you are changed and healed. Remember how many things came up during your early retrospection that you were amazed to find were still tangled up inside you. You sorted that out and were quite relieved and grateful for the help in healing those wounds and forgiving those hurts. Then you became a little discouraged at the new things that continuously came up and had to be faced as time moved on. There seemed to be no end to the problems and wounds that were revealed to you as you moved along the spiritual path.

Then as you approached the Illumination, you could look back at all the changes you went through letting go and letting go and you were grateful for the love you received and the strength and dedication of your teacher. You could not have foreseen the blessings you received at the Illumination and the sheer love that brought you into that experience. Your eyes opened a little to your teacher and you experienced their love and support for you. Then before long more darkness, bad habits and negative tendencies revealed themselves to you and you were discouraged yet again. You were a little frightened and began to ask if it is really possible for a human being to be problem free. Is it possible to ever really permanently change and be different? The answer from the teacher is always the same – of course you can and you will. You will be problem free, healed and changed over time. If you have the commitment, dedication and love, you will become who you were created to be. You will truly become your soul and Self.

It takes a tremendous amount of love to convince a soul to relax and trust the one leading them. It takes a superabundance of love to transform a living soul into a son or daughter of God, expressing the love, life and light that God intended for people. You will have to go through the fires of suffering for all of the errors and sins you have willfully committed. When you have submitted your anatomy to this purging and cleansing fire, you will experience the pure love of God washing you clean and burning out all of the dross. You have to work with the light for a while and do your exercises faithfully in order to increase in wisdom and understanding of yourself and others. You began to observe that each student is treated differently by the teacher depending on what their issues are, and you notice the priests attending in a loving and caring way that is profoundly patient and insightful. They seem to have this presence that does not think about them, but just about the person they are speaking with. You begin to wonder if you could love like that, teach like that or serve in that way. As you yearn to be useful, you begin to desire to serve and at the time you have no idea how you can be useful, but you long for that next step. You may be invited into deeper training and again will feel so new like you are starting over. You will feel so raised up and different that it will be humbling to be taught by the teacher. You will be floored by how direct the teacher is and sometimes intense in the way teachings are given to you. You might brace at first and then realized that no love would move if you tensed up, so you might just as well relax. The love that burns into you from the teacher causes whole new changes in your being that you could not have anticipated or dreamed of. The changes come swiftly and as you open, much more understanding and awareness opens within you. It is a stretch to watch how to help people, especially if you have lot of concepts about how things should be done or a lot of fears about safety and how to protect yourself and control everything. It dawns on you that you are being led through something you have no idea about.

So much love and patient guidance and teaching on the part of the teacher brings you to the place where you understand just a little of what a priest does and who they are growing to become. At this time the more insidious and stubborn personality flaws began to show themselves to the teacher. The long-standing attitudes and fears, the rigid holdings of your character and the deep-seated patterns from other lives begin to show up in you as you hold onto the old ways scraping against the teacher's suggestions and guidance. You get scared you might lose your accustomed habits and patterns and yet the love of the teacher presses you to give them up and be different. It takes a whole ton of love to move you off your little ledge, as you clutch it with a life and death fear thinking that the path and the teacher is forcing you to make a choice that will kill you. But the teacher has to press on you or you will never be any good for anyone. You have to let go if you are ever to be of any use to others and learn to love them in a universal and unconditional way, like Mary and Jesus do. You have to submit to the fire of their love if you are ever to be effective in moving souls to union with God. Your love has to have the mark of purity and patience stamped on you if you are to be able to be trusted with the souls that are being drawn into God through you.

The whole question of "How does God want me to be and express?" is new and startling. In the past, you worked on being an individual and some kind of unique phenomenal expression that would impress people. You were working on your moves and your style and how to be special instead of acting like a soul who had only God's intentions and desires. When the teacher is away, you get a taste of what it is like to serve and get out of the way and let the Spirit move through you. You start to learn that there is a universe of consciousness possible that you have barely conceived of as yet in the way of serving and knowing God. You are humbled and begin to have some necessary respect for the priesthood for the first time. You are humbled because you now realize how far you have to go to be that on and that responsible and conscious. You become excited because there is a way to become what you have seen from your elder brother and sisters who have come before you and obviously have succeeded in being able to serve in that deeper way.

You still listen in the counseling with the mind of the world and so are shocked at the teacher sometimes for not answering the questions in the way you think they should be answered. But you grow in trust of the process as you see the student moving along even though it is not what you thought should happen or what you would have said to cause them to move along. They move along because the Spirit is moving through the teacher who allows that guidance to come through while they are speaking with the student. The student can feel the love and learns to trust them with their life. This is a real spiritual school where there are teacher and students, master and disciples. That is the only way real spiritual development occurs, no matter what any bloated intellectual might tell you.

It takes a long time to figure out that the way people change is letting the love into their hearts and souls. In the beginning, you think it is the information given in the lesson that moves people along. Blessings and communion does accomplish magical changes and healings over time and moves people along spiritually. If you think about this for a minute, you might have noticed that some people come to class each weekand go to everything and still do not grow very much. They are choosing to not let go and have other gods inside them that are preventing them from turning their lives over to God. They have competing gods, so they just go through the motions which does not bring about transformation. The very simple teaching of Jesus that those who are forgiven much will be asked to do a lot is so true and powerful. The ones who are truly grateful for the forgiveness of their sins and who have let the love in the most are the ones who will devote their whole life in service to God out of gratitude and thankfulness. So when a student does not let go of much or let the forgiveness in very much, then I know I won't be able to count on them to serve very much or very long. It is really simple. The ones who let the love in will be the most loyal and reliable servants of God. Are you one of those? Can you let us love you completely? Or do you still hide your little fears and problems away to take them out on a lonely day and suckle them, feeding off the lie that they somehow comfort you? Are you still holding back and keeping a little bit for yourself? Because that is the selfishness that will take you down and pull you off the path.

It takes a whole lot of love to leaven the whole lump of clay. You have to be made pure so that when we offer you to people, you will be good food for starving souls. Because of the number of times you have received the Blood and Flesh of Jesus and Mary, you are gradually changed into another Jesus and Mary to be offered as a sacred substance for the souls yearning for grace. Do you know what a gift that is to become a living grace whose very substance could heal the world? Do you have any idea what Jesus and Mary are doing to you so that you become another Jesus and Mary for the earth?

You are the living Word of God sent down from Heaven. That means you are raised above the level of the earth so that you can be the essence of what each person needs in order to come into union with God. You are the life, light and love that have become grafted into the vine of Jesus and Mary in order to feed the spiritually hungry souls languishing here. Will you stand up and let the love in until you are so full that you never doubt again. That you are so lit up with light that you shine in every situation you walk into? Will you join us in heart and mind? It's take a whole lot of love.

REVIVAL

The world is against you trying to be spiritual. The people of the world are not much interested in virtue or holiness so few people will profess some longing for those things. People just want to have fun. They want to play, dance, enjoy themselves and be stimulated in whatever ways circumstances allow. For most people, if you can get something out life that pleases you, then you are doing better than most people. If you can take advantage of circumstances or other people and get things for yourself that others don't have, then it is to your credit. Spirituality is for those who are no fun and who have no hope of being lucky enough to get the most out of life. Spirituality is a word that is foreign to most people even if they use the word to describe something they think is better than religion. A lot more people consider themselves spiritual today because it seems more fashionable and interesting. But spirituality takes courage and boldness to go against the crowd and be different. If you are in the minority, you have to have greater courage to be that way than if you are one of the crowd. The multitudes, the crowds, are godless and anti-religious. They think that religious people are superstitious and lacking in fun and enjoyment. People think religious people are strange and backward, not up with the times or culturally aware. I am generalizing only a little. The people in Devon, England who came to my talks there referred to the UK as post-Christian. It seems like an appropriate description for millions of people who think Christianity is old and worn out, not relevant anymore in our sophisticated, civilized times. It does look like most people are not practicing any religious belief at all. There are Christians, Muslims, Jews and Hindus that hold fast to their religious upbringing in a culturally rigid way, meaning that they have never examined anything at all and just go along with the family flow. Certain things flow downhill. But for the most part, this cultural law to follow in the ancestral footsteps makes for less and less real spirituality and more and more shallow practice. There is no heart, no life in such practice and almost no examination of whether the practice works. In most cases, the religious customs just increase the bondage people have to a dead form that has lost its essence.

I think this is why religion is almost dead in the UK. Thinking people see it as shallow and not able to answer any real need. The hypocrisy of the ministers and priesthood has alienated people from a relationship with God and very few of the ministers actually have a real, spiritual connection to God. Most of them have an intellectual head full of ideas that are concepts and not an actual devotional or contemplative relationship with God at the center of being. I don't think we are post Christian, I think we have not had a majority on earth ever become really Christian. Real Christians are few and far between as it would take a clear transformation of heart, mind and soul to follow Christ. Jesus Christ would not recognize most of what passes in the world for Christian. He might see more Buddhists acting like Christians. But that is mythology as well since most members of other religions have the same degree of hypocrisy as the Christians. They say the right words and act an entirely different way. They talk love without really demonstrating love through their thought and actions.

In the U.S. people claim to be Christian but are unable to forgive someone when they are wronged. They become mean and aggressive when wronged and act like animals when people do not conform to how they feel one should act or think. The level of aggressive intolerance in the U.S. is extreme and exactly opposite of what Jesus taught. He taught understanding, peace, compassion and consideration for each other. He taught no killing, no hating and no lusting. How many people can actually keep those negative desires from rising to the surface and acting out? How many can actually never have those thoughts at all?

You see how far we are from actually being like Christ – Christians? It is not easy to follow Jesus and Mary because to be like them, you have to change almost everything in you. You cannot be like people of the world who take no thought and have no care for others unless they are part of their clan. Jesus taught that all people are our neighbors, not just our family or the people from our own town.

I was in Ashburton, England at the Methodist Church. They have about 15 regulars and on a good day maybe 25 people attending. There is a core group of about 6 people who pray regularly and attend often and have meals together. The minister has to attend to 5 other churches in the surrounding area and is stretched pretty thin. But it is convenient for the minister because they don't have to really get to know the people that much and don't really have time to know them very well. They are figure heads that don't really teach. They just do the baptisms, weddings and funerals and then once a month they commemorate communion. Getting people into the church is hard and most of them are older. The same was the case in Exeter, a much bigger city where there were only about 25 people as regular attendees and then most of them older. Very few younger people were being attracted to the church and that is the case all over Europe. What it looks like is that the Churches are dusting over with oldness and becoming relics in the process of becoming museums while no new young people are coming in to participate. It is not hard to see why – there is no real food being served to people. The ministers are only taught academic knowledge and have no deep or real experience of God other than their head knowledge. That is true for 95% of them. The few that might have a real relationship with God have a shallow one due to never being taught by a real teacher and not having access to a real relationship with God. No one taught them how and there was no one around to show them what that was supposed to look like. So the churches are dying and hardly anyone is being drawn into a spiritual life anymore. This is a sad plight for the whole world. Jesus and Mother Mary are just as unappreciated today as in the past and it does not look like people want anything to do with them.

We have a very big job to do on this planet. We have to revive the spiritual life of people through our own example. We will not be able to do it through the common means of church groups and church meetings. We will have to do it cell by cell; small group by small group, one at a time. A cell is a small group under 25 people that comes together and thoroughly knows each other and learns to commune together under special principles and practices. We have devised such small cells where people can be real with one another and learn how to be in loving and considerate relations with each other. There can be no back-biting, no hypocrisy or expressions of animosity. People have to serve each other with love. We have to love one another like Jesus and Mary love us. We have to put our sisters and brothers needs before our own. We have to be patient with those who have not learned how to love yet and teach them by example. We have to revive the sacraments in the full power and grace because they are almost lost. The priesthood has to take the place of shallow pastors and ministers. A real priest teaches individual students the spiritual path and how to function as a God being and get over their problems. A real priest is a dynamic healer of the nations and the people and someone to look up to who is well beyond the development of most people. We train ones in such a capacity and with such a consciousness. Consciousness teaches, not head knowledge. Consciousness transforms the world, not academic conditioning. People want real answers to questions and not dogma. Those who want anything real at all will not settle for shallow truths or a leader who does not know anything spiritually. You have to know and not merely repeat the words of those who do.

You have to become such a person who others can follow and look up. Your spiritual example must inspire others to want to come to that place of consciousness themselves.

What it looks like on the planet is that most of the Christian world is collapsing in a sea of hopelessness and numbness. The churches are empty because people aren't seeking God anymore. The churches are emptying because the ministers are not examples of what they are reading or speaking. When this happens, a whole culture and society is on the decline and soon comes to a desperate end. Even if your life on earth does end, if you have a real spiritual connection and love for God, you will not be disillusioned when the hard times come like a wind out of hell. You will remember God and Jesus and Mary and not have to feel so lost while those around you fall into so much terror and fear. Come learn with us and let us teach you and you will never regret it.

THE JOY OF SUFFERING

Do you still get mad when things don't go the way you want them to go? Do you find yourself getting upset when you are not given the respect that you feel is due or the recognition that you deserve? How long can you stand having things go against you before you react and lash out at something? Isn't it because you feel that you have put up with a situation or a person for long enough and you think that there should be a limit to such trouble? A person of your magnitude, your stature and intelligence should not have to put up with situations like this, isn't that right? You should be above all of these challenges and limitations and not have to be inconvenienced by the people that make these situations happen, isn't that right?

In most cases, these limitations are designed to test you and make you aware of yourself and your capacity. If you take a deeper look at what purpose these situations serve, you will see that it is an answer to a prayer that you made. Didn't you ask God to show you the way? Haven't you asked that you be brought closer to a real experience of God? Didn't you make that prayer recently that Jesus or Mary show you what was in you that stood in your way of experiencing real light, real love and real peace? These situations are given to you to show you how much you have to learn, how much you have to let go of and how much you have to open in order to be able to have that prayer answered by God. God is answering your prayer and showing you how much you resist light, love and peace. You said you wanted those things. You prayed for them and in some cases, even demanded them. Then God answered your prayer by giving you a situation that would test your resolve to be the way you asked to be, the experience you wanted to grow into. You failed the test. As it happens, students fail the tests many times before they see how simple everything is and how important every thought, desire and reaction is.

Every reaction reveals what you feel is important. If your pride is important to you, then you will be extremely reactive and angry most of the time. You might oscillate from anger to hurt on the roller coaster of emotions. Everything that people say and do, each situation outside you, has the power to make you feel a certain way. You let the outside control your inside environment. You have not become an environmentalist yet. You still exercise no control over your inner temperament or emotions. Everything and everybody else controls you and you are tossed around by all the winds of fate like a feather in a breeze. If you want to be in light, then you have to be shining and maintaining that shininess in the face of storms or clouds going on around you. If you want to be the epitome of love, then you have to respond to everything and everyone with love or you will be doing something entirely different. If you want to be the experience of peace, you have to respond peaceably to everything and everyone as a habit of your being. Then you will need to discipline yourself to not allow any agitation, anger, hurt or fear to disturb the waters of your heart. If you want peace, then you have to emanate peace. You have to personify peace.

Consistency is not easy. Consistency will cause you to suffer because you have to maintain a pattern in order to be consistent. You cannot say that one day you want to be all peace, love and light and the next day forget about it and do whatever you want. Because you cannot build up strength in a new pattern without consistency and discipline. Discipline means you train yourself to become what you want to be, what you want to express. Consistency is one of the most difficult things to learn for any student. It means you are going to suffer the loss of the old pattern. It means that all the old options die and that causes suffering and death. You suffer because you decided to be different. People expect you to act the same as you always have and so they are startled if not offended when you act differently. You suffer in their reaction because sometimes they get mad at you. You suffer in their reaction because they expect you to relate the way you have always related and when you don't they are shocked or angry that you have changed. Every time you make a change, someone is going to be upset with you. You can either resist change and be miserable or you can change and experience other people's upset. But changing and accepting what will come your way from others is the better way as the suffering will only last for a short time in reality.

When will you understand the joy of suffering? You will enter into the joy of suffering when you feel the love of Jesus, Mary and God and it no longer matters to you what people think about you. People are fickle and will react to you according to the way the wind blows. If the barometric pressure is right and the weight of gravity is not heavy on their liver, then you might get a response that is accepting of you and your changes. In another climate, people can turn on you and accuse you of anything and it will burn a little. But if you have turned the corner and really felt the love of God in your body, you no longer find those accusations or criticisms important or meaningful. You let them slide off your back like water streaming off a duck that rises up out of the lake. Those criticisms do not reach the depths of your being. But God's love has touched you there and nothing in the outer world can compare to it. You suffer because of the misunderstandings and meanness of others, but you have felt the love of Jesus and Mary and you are not dismayed by any fleeting whim of human beings.

You can enter more and more into love, light and peace as you stop looking outside for recognition and acceptance from human beings. Your sisters and brothers in the spiritual life do accept you and have been taught to accept people as souls and so you can count on that. But you may have traits of character that are so intolerable that your brothers and sisters, out of love for you, have to confront you with these bad habits to help you rid yourself of them. It is not a negative judgment, but a positive affirmation of your true being that they will hold for you the affirmation of your true nature, even when you are not aware of that as yet. It is suffering letting someone love you when you don't know yourself yet. They see you clearly and you only see yourself as in an opaque mirror vaguely. You suffer in the transition from your awkward self into your true self. Your metamorphose from the hunk of flesh that you have pretended to be into the butterfly of your soul. It is a struggle and there is so much joy because the struggle is worth it and you become more truly who you really are.

I want all of you to start opening to the joy of suffering. I am not talking about being a martyr which some of you have master's degrees in. I am not talking about acting pious and tortured. I am not talking about being morbid. I am recommending that you start to enjoy being stretched, that you appreciate the awkwardness of not knowing who you are while your teacher sees what is happening inside of you and you don't. I am talking about being in joy while you are molting and changing and when you have no idea what you will turn into. I want you to offer up your trials as a small little portion of suffering that you can enter into in honor of what Jesus experienced.

I want to relate a story of St. Francis and Brother Leo.
One winter day Francis was coming to St. Mary of the Angels from Perugia with Brother Leo, and the bitter cold made them suffer keenly. St Francis called to Brother Leo, who was walking a bit ahead of him, and said: 'Brother Leo, even if all the brothers in every country give a great example of holiness and integrity and testify well, nevertheless write down and not carefully that perfect joy is not in that. If all the masters in theology in Paris joined our order, write: that is not true joy. Or all the prelates

beyond the mountains – archbishops and bishops, of the Kings of France and England joined our order – write: that is not true joy. Or if the brothers went to the unbelievers and converted all of them to the faith; or that I have so much grace from God that I heal the sick and perform miracles; I tell you that true joy is not in all those things.

And when he walked on a bit St Francis called him again, saying" "Brother Leo, even if the brothers give sight to the blind, heal the paralyzed, drive out devils, give hearing back to the deaf, make the lame walk, and restore speech to the dumb, and what is still more, bring back to life a man who has been dead four days, write that perfect joy is not in that."

And going on for a while, Francis cried out again in a strong voice: "Brother Leo, if a brother knew all languages and all sciences and scripture, if he also knew how to prophesy and to reveal not only the future but also the secrets of consciences and minds of others, write down and not carefully that perfect joy is not in that."

And as they walked on, after a while Francis called again forcefully: "Brother Leo, little lamb of God, even if a brother could speak with the voice of an angel, and know the courses of the stars and the powers of herbs, and knew all about the treasures in the earth, and if he knew the qualities of birds and fishes, animals, humans, roots, trees, rocks, and waters, write down and not carefully that true joy is not in that."And going on a bit further, Francis called again strongly" "Brother Leo, even if a brother could preach so well that he should convert all infidels to the faith of Christ, write that perfect joy is not there."

Now when the had been talking this way for a distance of two miles, Brother Leo in great amazement asked him: "Father, I beg you in God's name to tell me where perfect joy is."

St. Francis replied: "When we come to St. Mary of the Angels, soaked by the rain and frozen by cold, all soiled with mud and suffering hunger, and we ring at the gate of tho place and the brother porter says angrily: "Who are you?" and we say: "We are two of your brothers." And he contradicts us, saying: "You are not telling the truth. Rather, you are two rascals who go around deceiving people and stealing what they give to the poor. Go away." And he does not open for us, but makes us stand outside in the snow and rain, cold and hungry, until night falls – then if we endure all those insults and cruel rebuffs patiently, without being troubled and without complaining, and if we reflect humbly and charitably that that porter really knows us and that God makes him speak against us, oh, Brother Leo, write, that perfect joy is there."

"And if we continue to knock, and the porter comes out in anger, and drives us away with curses and hard blows like bothersome scoundrels, saying: "Get away from here, you dirty thieves, go to the hospital. Who do you think you are? You certainly won't eat or sleep here." And if we bear it patiently and take the insults with joy and love in our hearts, oh, Brother Leo, write that that is perfect joy."

"And if later, suffering intensely from hunger and painful cold, with night falling, we still knock and call, and crying loudly beg them to open for us and let us come in for the love of God, and he grows still more angry and says: 'Those fellows are bold and shameless ruffians. I'll give then what they deserve." And he comes out with a knotty club, and grasping us by the cowl throws us onto the ground, rolling us in the mud and snow, and beats us with that club so much that he covers our bodies with wounds, if we endure all those evils and insults and blows with joy and patience, reflecting that we must accept and bear the sufferings of the Blessed Christ patiently for love of him, oh Brother Leo, write: that is perfect joy."

64

"And now hear the conclusion, Brother Leo. Above all the graces and gifts of the Holy Spirit which Christ gives to his friends is that of conquering oneself and willingly enduring sufferings, insults, humiliations, and hardships for the love of Christ. For we cannot glory in all those other marvelous gifts of God, as they are not ours but God's, as the Apostle says: What have you that you have not received?" But we can glory in the cross of tribulations and afflictions, because that is ours, and so the Apostle says: "I will not glory save in the Cross of Our Lord Jesus Christ."

JOY IN THE WORLD

The wonders of nature are revealed in the rising Sun, the sounds of leaves rustling, the active life of birds, animals and plants. The myriad creatures and the magnificent foliage brings awe and reverence for a creation so organized and ordered that only God could have made all of this. I know science has explanations in their limited and narrow view of life. Science has joined with the Church to persecute those who were inspired by nature and acknowledged God as the one cause of everything.

When I was young, I was awed by nature and spent most of my waking life outdoors exploring and seeing everything. I lived near the ocean for half of my childhood and would wade in the streams of a large marsh near the ocean. I would search for minnows and crayfish; we called them crawdads, and anything alive swimming in the clear brackish water. The marsh was a few hundred yards wide stretched along a half mile of beach. It was mostly grasses and was thick with twenty inches of mud when one walked into it. Otherwise there was board walk about 12 inches wide that one could walk along all the way across it if you were heading for the beach and sand. So many things were alive in that marsh, it was teaming with life. I was in awe of how much was going on there and I would spend days and hours watching and exploring. If I wanted a different adventure I would bring my deep-sea fishing pole down to the Narragansett Bay and cast off shore for flounder. The flounder lie in the sand off shore and would bite on worms or periwinkles that I found under some rocks by the shore. I would actually use anything for bait, but the flounder liked the periwinkles and sea worms, if I could save up money that I earned from chores. I would also swim for hours and hours along the shore looking for living things to observe. The world was full of wonder for me and it was like living in paradise. All of creation was fascinating and exciting.

People were interesting too, but not nearly as nice or safe as the creatures I would find in the natural world. You never knew what people were going to do, whether they were in a bad mood or whether they were mean. But outside in nature, everything was wondrous, splendid and exciting. I remember discovering a special area of an overgrown area near the train tracks below my house on the hill where there were these huge vines growing. They were like a sea of vines, all soft and strong at the same time. I could climb them and roll on top of them and nest in them as a look out where I could barely be seen, but had a view of everything and anyone walking around. I would climb on these and play on top of them with my friends for hours and hours. I was thrilled to be experiencing so beautiful a scene and to be so loved by nature and so supported. The world was exciting and mysterious at the same time. What great intelligence made so beautiful these scenes with thousands of textures, colors, sounds and smells? It was so exhilarating. There was no end to the variety and no boredom whatsoever. I was in a paradise that God created and I was in joy to be in the world. I really, really liked it on this planet.

I know many of you can remember when you were thrilled on this earth by a sunset, a stream, a pool of quiet waters or a flower or a breeze with the wind blowing the grasses or a hot quiet afternoon with only the sound of dragon flies buzzing the horizon. Everything becomes quiet and still and there is a feeling of being at peace and being completely taken care of. There is no desiring or striving or wanting or worrying. It is all stillness and there is the thrill of life creating all around you. So many memories, so many moments of being completely in the wonder of creation. Artist and poets have captured these moments in verse and couplets, touching into a presence that could be called God.

But most people do not want to give any credit to such a powerful being as God. They want to understand the material world as separate, random and accidental. They prefer to let science describe things instead of appreciate where this all was dreamed up. God's mind dreamed all of this up. There is a much higher joy than the joys that are evident and able to be experienced in the natural world.

The world can offer you beautiful scenery, wonders of nature, experiences with people and places to be. The world can have joys that are quite magnificent and expansive. People can be loving and understanding. In times of crisis, human beings demonstrate heroic love and compassion and they rise above the tribal loyalties of race, country or religion and really love others. But humans day to day are not always kind or helpful. Sometimes they are mean and nasty. Sometimes they hate and kill either a body or a reputation. But life has sunny days and rainy days, clouds and storms as well as calm. The joys of the world are intense and meaningful. When a baby is born, or a child cries; when thunder cracks the sky or a bird crashes to death against a clear window pane; when a mother comforts her child and shows pure love and giving or an angry person steals something from someone – these experiences imprint us with sadness and hope. Some of us will move into the giving sphere. Some of us will stay in the world of hatred and anger. Even if we are enjoying ourselves today, who is to say whether the way we are living is going to reap eternal joy or eternal torment.

Is your joy going to be eternal? To be eternal, you have to be unattached to the outcome. For your joy to be eternal, you would have to see that the joys the world can offer do not last and cannot fulfill permanently. Things change and no beautiful moment lasts forever. So the joys of the world do not last. Most people try to create things that will last. If you have ever bought something kind of cheap, like a piece of clothing, where it was not made well and not made with quality materials. It looks good for a few washings and then it fades or the stitching starts to pull out or frazzles. Whereas, if you buy something of quality, you can enjoy it for quite some time. The only trouble is that you might get tired of it. I usually buy cars when styles change and there are new technologies and upgrades like GPS or electric, fuel-efficient innovations that mean something environmentally. I enjoy technological advances, but there are hundreds of them each year in our lives now and it would necessitate many new purchases each year. That becomes impractical since my joy would diminish as my charge card debt increases. So I have to be balanced in my joys as well. Some joys are obtained at too high a cost and will actually cause sadness.

Too many good things make people rot. Too much wealth makes many people paranoid of other people and suspicious that people will try to take their wealth. More and more refined foods cause the palate to shut down and not be able to taste the refinements any longer. If you smell roses all the time, your olfactory sense shuts down and you cannot smell them anymore because you have been overwhelmed with the scent of roses. The joys of this world are best experienced in season and at timely moments so that you can appreciate them. It is in the contrasts that one is most truly able to enjoy the moment. If all the moments were the same, life would get boring. This is one of the teachings about things being impermanent and ever-changing. In the swirling of the experiences of the world and the material life everything changes. In God everything remains the same and does not change.

If your goal in life is to experience joy in the world, then you will have many moments of joy and there will be exquisite experiences of profound meaning and purpose. You will have highs and lows like most creatures great and small who live in the material world. You will have moments of great love from other people and towards other people. It won't last, however. Because people cannot keep up consistently with hardly anything that is important. People are mostly fickle and suffer from sadness, fears and longing. It is a rare individual that can stay centered in the face of a hurricane or be still when people are dying or maintain peace in the face of persecution. The world has all of these things: death, suffering, beauty and laughter; illness and pleasure; abundance and deprivation; healing and health; compassion and anger. So many things. You could actually try to achieve as much worldly joy as possible and spend all of your time trying to stay in beautiful experiences. But you would be moving more and more into trying very hard to stay in those experiences. You might have to be vigilant about what will take you out of joy and who might interfere with your joys. You would have to be thinking more and more about yourself in order to be undisturbed by others who might not have your joy in mind. In this protected state, you could not be open to whatever experiences came along. You could not be content with whatever life dishes out to you because you are convinced that joy should be your state in life. Then you might get angry at those who do not have your joy as their goal for you. You might be upset when things don't go as planned. You might get so selfish thinking about your own personal joy that you have no time for anyone else, since they have another, different agenda. You can see how out of balance you would get if your goal was your own personal joy.

When I was a younger boy, I marveled at each new discovery and engaged in life thoroughly and completely. I worked hard and looked carefully at everything. I played hard with my three dogs and three cats. I built forts and blew up things and made a mark on the environment in hundreds of ways. There was no tree that had not been climbed or body of water that had not had a raft built in order to cross over it. Everything was a huge playground of adventure and I was in joy most of the time. When I came home was when the trouble started. The contrast between nature and home was striking. One week I gathered drift wood that would be driven into shore by the autumn storms and hurricanes that lashed the coastline. My friend and I made a complete one room house from everything that I found and some tools and nails that I borrowed from my father. The house would have stood for some time. We had many meals in that house. We made fires by the shore and brought down tinfoil and butter to wrap the fish that we caught from the Bay. We took naps there sometimes to recuperate from wild adventuring. But the neighbors started complaining because a whole bunch of mice started to move in under the floor boards and also they did not like their shoreline view disturbed by this little house on the beach. So we had to burn it to the ground. Our joy was in the building and using that house. Our sadness was the anger of the neighbors that it had to be torn down. Such are the ups and downs of joy in the material world.

Jesus said, "In the world you will have tribulation. But behold, I have overcome the world." There is an inner place inside you that is undisturbed by anything that happens in the material world. No storm, no adverse circumstance, no hostility from others, no disease of body or worry in mind will change the peace that resides deep within the human soul. When you are still and no longer reacting to circumstance, you can rest there and experience the peace that Jesus taught. He overcame the allurements and attachments to the world and thus was able to manifest complete peace and love in a perfect balance. So don't be fooled into thinking that the world should serve you up course after course of joy, bliss and wonder. You will have moments of that because God wants to remind you that the only real and lasting bliss and wonder is in union with God. All joys in the world are temporary when compared with the inner joy of union with God.

THE JOY OF STRETCHING

Have you observed a cat getting up from a long nap? They stretch their front paws out and then their little fingers and the claws come out a bit and then they raise up their back and stretch that and then finally they elongate one back leg at a time and stretch those out. This is all to get the body ready to move around and be agile and limber and get the blood moving again after a little sleeping. They seem to enjoy the process although attributing human emotions of joy might be a little too much projecting onto the simple cat brain. Anyway, stretching is preparatory to moving. In the same way, stretching is preliminary to a change in energy.

For example, if you are going to run, exercise or work out, you are advised to stretch and prepare the body for strenuous exercise. You stretch the muscles and remove all tightness so the muscles can work more fluidly and gracefully. In the same way, if you are preparing to meditate, you shake off any sleep, which is a form of stretching so that your mind is alert and you are ready to enter into communion with God. You make yourself still and one-pointed by shedding the emotions, worries, fears and concerns of daily life. You cannot meditate unless you stretch out of where you have been and prepare yourself for where you are going. You do this in mind. If you are going to do some writing on the computer, you will have to get yourself in the state of mind of sitting for some period of time, and concentrating on the subject of your writing. You have to stretch out of how you were thinking and feeling beforehand so that you can enter in and commit completely to the process of writing. The same is true if you want to have a conversation with someone. You have to prepare your mind and heart to open and be willing to attend fully to the other person so that you can be really with them while you listen and talk to each other. This takes stretching and changing the way you were functioning beforehand into a good conversationalist and listener with people.

You have to get very efficient at changing gears and moving from one kind of action and behavior to another without any jerking and sputtering. Some of you still sputter, spew and fume when you have to shift gears between demands from your environment. Some of you have set ideas of how long things should take and how irritated you allow yourself to be when something comes along to disturb your complacency or your scheduled event. Many times you fall into such habit patterns of behavior that any change in venue brings up fears of never getting what you want or anger that people interfere so disrespectfully. You have to get over yourself and realize that life is a series of changing scenes and necessities. Nothing lasts forever in the material world and it is supposed to be that way. Flow with the changes and let God move you along through the many different facets of life. You can't eat all the time. You can't sleep all the time. You can't meditate all the time. You can't work all the time. I know it's irritating. But life is not made of only planting. There is also weeding and watering; weeding and harvesting. There is also winter when no weeding, planting or harvesting can be done. Everything must be in its own season and each action when it is right.

I know some of you have been so spoiled by life that you want everything exactly when you want it. You cannot wait patiently until the time is right for an action or a benefit. You have been so hurt that you have to have everything yesterday because to delay any gratification is like having to die. Some of you get so mad about this kind of thing that you threaten everyone around you with leaving or through your bad moods. You inflict hurt on those around you because they don't comply with your wishes and don't feel obligated to help you relieve your anger at important people. I want my sleep now. I want my alone time now. I want to have fun now. I want my food and dessert now. I want my payback now for wrongs done to me. I want. I want. I want. All the little babies of the world unite on this one point: I was wronged and want everyone or anyone close to me to pay. There is no feeling that you can wait patiently for God to make things right. There is very little forgetting about the hurts and forgiving them and letting life take care of you the way life will take care of you. God takes care of every creature under Heaven.

It stretches you to get out of the way and let life teach you something. It stretches you to have to own your faults and admit them to others without bracing or fearing reprisals. It stretches you to open to love even when you are convinced that you will be hurt again. This is when stretching hurts and is painful. Opening to being taken care of or loved is not your customary pattern, so it hurts because you have to trust something bigger than you. You have to allow God to guide the process which stretches you out of your accustomed pattern of running the show and controlling everyone around you by your demands and moods. Stretching hurts sometimes because you are being asked on the spiritual path to open to things you don't know and to ways of being that you are not accustomed to. You are being asked to give until it hurts. You are being asked to give up bad habits that are killing you and replacing those with abstract things, like new thoughts and feelings. We ask you to open where you were formerly closed. We ask you to try different things whereas before you were not open to consider those. We ask you to love people that you wouldn't naturally gravitate towards. We stretch you into opening to all people because formerly you were strangled by your little tribe believing your loyalty to them would give you peace and happiness.

Loyalty to tribe, to family, to country, to religion will strangle your soul and make you fickle and mean to whole populations of human beings. We do not want you limited in your love for all human beings. So we stretch you past your usual and customary acceptances or you cannot be a real disciple of Jesus and Mary. You are to have no loyalty higher than God. The next is loyalty to yourself, then to your teacher and then to your spiritual community. Since we are a spiritual order, we are like the monasteries and convents of days gone by, except that we are monastics living among the people of the world and not cloistered away from others. We are to live like we are living in a spiritual community as an example to all in the world who do not know how to live and are miserable in their mind and flesh. We are dedicated to establish a new way of living where God is first and the spiritual community is the most powerful connection before all other relationships. We are dedicated to stretch the conceptions of the world mind so that they will learn that a life in God and in spiritual community is more real, more alive, more loving, more peaceful and more dynamic than anything they can experience. We want to entice them into this life.

What will entice them? We will shine like the Sun. Our light will be our signature and it will be recognized by everyone because of the vitality of our feelings, the light in our body and eyes, the health of our minds and the power of our energy. They will feel the most outstanding signature of our discipleship to Jesus and Mary – our love. This love will pervade every disciple in our spiritual community and it will be palpable and intense. There is nothing as powerful as love and nothing so protective and inviting. We invite people into this love. That is our mission. But the consequences are that people will have to leave their old life of anger, hatred, fear and separation from God. We will gradually stretch their hearts open to love more and more until they are burned up on the fire of love and spend themselves thoroughly in the blaze of love in adoration to God. Each disciple must be this way and learn to stretch into being so aflame with God's presence that people will know you by that energy, that signature. Everything else means nothing. How much you know means nothing. How many useless words you utter means nothing, and in fact, almost always overwhelms and makes it harder to accept love. The more you engage the thinking, the more nuances one's pride has to consider. Pride of mind is exactly what we want to avoid. Some of you still think getting things right is a spiritual attribute. Some of you still think too much and are prideful about those little mental droppings that pass as thought in your brain. The more attached you are to your ideas and opinions, the less love you will give and the less light you will shine.

Suffering is not fun. The world says suffering is bad. But actually suffering is part of every relationship. Every time you put out any effort and anytime you are stretched in consciousness, you suffer a little. The goal of worldly people is to have no pain and no suffering. They want a life of ease and happiness. They are willing to do almost anything to get the easy life. Usually having the goal of coasting through life will create the most pain possible as everything in your life will turn into endless pain and suffering. Waiting for life to dish up for you a platter of beautiful experiences just because you crave them, will not be successful. You have to put yourself in the place of being able to receive those things in order for it to be possible to have them. The cost of having things your way will cancel love and separate you from God. We will, we will stretch you.

Many of you can attest to the fact that when you first began training, you had very rigid ideas of how much work you could do, how long you could persist at a task, how much rest you needed, etc. You even portioned out your efforts to suit your past history of practically no life force moving in you. You would anticipate hours of rest after small doses of effort. You would pine for days off and ways to hide from responsibilities. You would laze out when the teacher was away. In this way you were actually taking a needed break since there was always more asked of you and from your limited perspective, you were already being stretched pretty thin. If you mentioned how hard you were working the teacher would kind of half smile with sympathy for your lack of understanding and encourage you to stretch your capacity for life moving through you. In some cases we had to get the paddles for all clear and zap you with energy so that you would show some vital signs again.

It is a fact that you are capable of so much more. It is a fact that God wants to move much, much more energy and love, life and light through you. If you let this happen, you will come alive and be amazed that you were even able to describe what you experienced before as living. You have the capacity that Jesus or Mother Mary had and you need to expand your awareness to encompass a much greater capacity that God will make possible in you.

Come join us and allow us to remake your world and refashion you in the image of God.

SLOTH VERSUS DILIGENCE

Sloth is defined as indolence, an aversion to work or exertion, laziness and slow moving. In more pristine forests, the animal, the sloth, lives in the trees and comes down every few days for water. It is exceptionally slow moving almost imperceptibly. It is an apt symbol for how some people move their bodies and motivate their minds. Indolence, laziness and idleness are synonyms for sloth but with a slightly different feeling. Indolence means inactive and disinclined to exert oneself. Laziness is resistance to work, sluggish. And idleness is avoidance of work. In each of these descriptions is a decision not to move quickly and not to be jostled into making much of an effort.

The mass mind support for this negative energy is the idea that life is hard and there is so much hardship, pain and suffering, that it is only natural to want to take breaks and get some relief. Is life hard? Have you worked that hard? Have you been stretched lately by needing to apply an intense effort at something? This tendency to take breaks and to reward oneself with time off begins very early with the rewards and strokes that we are given for making small efforts as children. We are celebrated for miniscule effort and complemented for any improvements in our behavior. Sometimes this creates a condition where you don't know what is important inside yourself, except by what the environment or people outside you want from you. Then to please them for rewards, you sort of lose your internal perspective and what is important to you. The malaise of pleasing others weakens your own imagination and you no longer know what is important to you and so just live by the demands of other people and how to garner their approval. As this condition becomes pervasive, you also lose your internal motivation to do things because of what you want to do. The situation grows to making sure you do just what you are told and just as much as you are expected to do. The comments with siblings of "that's not my job," and "she doesn't have to, so why should I?" become commonplace.

If you have not made any of your own decisions, then you will eventually resent other people making decisions for you. You will pay them back for what they took from you perhaps unconsciously resenting them while it was you who did not decide what you wanted and so boycotted all cooperation. When a person has a slowness to cooperate with others, they are mad. They are taking their anger out on other people or on the situation. The most passive way to act out anger is to go slower or to forget to help at all. This is very effective in making everyone around you angry, but they are angry at you for not cooperating and not helping. That is aggressive and mean, even though it looks like you forgot or were successfully pre-occupied with other things. It is actually conscious on your part and you have been paying someone back for forcing you to work or to make a contribution or to do what they wanted you to do.

Being averse to working and moving slowly are extremely angry actions. They come from an entitlement that you should be exempt from such things or have suffered enough to take a big life-long break. If you resist work or try to run and hide when big projects are required, then you are saying to the people who might be counting on you that you are above them or are angry with them for asking you to help. You might be furious that they don't see that other people should be getting their hands dirty and you have had enough of that from mom and dad.

The opposite of sloth is diligence. Diligence is defined as decisive work ethic, enthusiasm, and budgeting one's time to guard against laziness. It involves an earnest and persistent application in an undertaking. It involves steady effort and attentive care. There is present with diligence a painstaking, persevering effort. A synonym is the word busy. A decisive work ethic is that you jump into what needs to be done without any hesitation and you persist to completion of the task at hand. There is no resistance to work, no sloth in other words. There is no inactivity or avoidance of work. There is no trace of going slow so others will have to pick up the slack and take care of things that you are not attending to or don't want to do. Also lacking in diligence, is the tendency to feel overwhelmed or slighted by the efforts that are required to get a job done.

If you are diligent, you will jump in quickly and move your body as fast as possible without considering how long you will have to work. I used to ask the laziest person in the restaurant to figure out how to do a job and then write a job description of that task. I would observe the labor saving moves the person would do in order to not work very hard. They would do things in the least amount of steps possible because they did not want to exert any more effort or move their body any more steps than was absolutely necessary. Many times these employees would manage to cut out a few extra steps and save time for everyone. But it was selfish and based on sloth rather than any diligent effort or feeling of integrity to the job. Moving slowly is a direct sign of anger and hatred. If you move slowly, you can be assured that you are angry at some important people in your life. There is no other way around it. If you are slow moving, you are mad. If you don't put out much effort, if you save yourself from anything hard, you are stuck in anger and pride. We will talk about pride later. But it is important to note that pride is the root of many of the vices and negative emotions and actions.

If you save yourself all the time, if you spread out the effort so that you are not exhausted, then you are calculating your gains and losses. You are making sure you manage your energy to have something left over for yourself at the end of the job. That means you are averse to exertion and avoiding work. If you avoid work, you are saying that your body should be treated more specially and you should pamper the flesh as it has had a hard enough time already. There is no enthusiasm in such behavior, as you are more vigilant to how much is being taken out of your hide than how much you can give. Remember Jesus' words, "It is more blessed to give than to receive." What you put out you get back. If your prayer is to make life easy and get enough money to go on vacation for the rest of your days, then life will be taken from you. A fairly recent example was a man in his early thirties who wanted to work two more years and then retire to some tropical island and sun himself on the beach all day. I was amazed that a grown up person would have as a goal to withdraw from life and then coast into oblivion for the rest of his life. It was sad. A few months later he had a very serious motorcycle accident and was paralyzed from the waste down. His life was now indolent as he could no longer work or make any effort physically at all. He has to be taken care of for the rest of his life, which was the answer to his prayer. So be careful what you pray for because you will have an answer to your prayer. He wanted to not work, so now he can't.

LAZINESS

Vol. 2, p. 225

"In some places the land was still covered with stubble and couch-grass, an arid hard land, encumbered with parasite plants, the seeds of which had been carried there from the desert waste by the summer winds. They were the fields of lazy and fast-living people. In other places the soil had already been turned by the ploughshare, and stones, bramble and couch-grass had been cleared away by fire and man's toil. And what before was harmful, that is the useless plants, were turned by the purifying fire and man's toil into good manure and useful fertilizing salts. The soil may have suffered because of the pain caused by the share that cut into

it and rummaged through it, and because of the biting fire that scorched its wounds. But it will rejoice in spring, more beautiful, saying: "Man tortured me to give me these rich crops, which make me beautiful." And they were the fields of willing people. And in other places the soil was already soft, also the ashes had been cleared away, it was a real nuptial bed for its fertile union to the seed that gives so many glorious ears of wheat. And they were the fields of people who were so generous as to reach perfection in activity. Well, the same applies to hearts. I am the share and my Word is the Fire, to prepare men for the eternal triumph."

Vol. 3, p. 470
"Would you perhaps expect the sea to make havoc in its depths by means of furious storms to detach pearl-oysters from their beds and open them by the striking power of billows and thus offer them on the shore to lazy people who do not want to work, to cowards who do not want to run risks? Would you expect the earth to make trees out of grains of sand and give you fruit without any seed? No, my dear. Fatigue, work and courage are required. And above all, no prejudices."

Vol. 4, p.371
"But do you not know that once you have laid your hand on the plough you must persevere for one, ten, one hundred years, as long as your life lasts, because to stop is a crime against oneself, as one denies oneself a greater glory, and it is a regression, because generally he who stops not only does not proceed further, but turns back? The treasure of Heaven must increase year by year to be good. Because if Mercy is benign to those also who had few years to store it up, it will not be an accomplice of lazy people who in a long life do little. It is a treasure increasing continuously. Otherwise it is no longer a fruit-bearing treasure, but an unfruitful one, which is detrimental to the readily available peace of Heaven."

83

Vol. 4, p.454

"But we have within us passions, which are like citizens closed within the circle of town walls. It is necessary for all the passions of men to want the same thing: that is, holiness. Otherwise some will tend to Heaven in vain, if others leave the doors unguarded and let the seducer enter or counteract the actions of part of the spiritual citizens through disputes or laziness, making the interior part of the town perish and abandoning it to nettles, poison, couch grass, snakes, scorpions, mice, jackals and owls, that is to wicked passions and to Satan's angels. You must be unceasingly vigilant, like sentries placed at the walls, to prevent the Evil one from entering where we want to build the Kingdom of God."

Vol. 5, p. 408

"The gifts of God are not common ordinary things, they are special ones. One cannot claim them nor can one become lazy and say: 'God will give them to me.' It is written: "You shall eat bread moistened with the sweat of your forehead," that is the bread earned through hard work."

Vol. 8, p. 137

"The same happens to those who descend spiritually instead of ascending. One's virtue and wisdom become more and more limited and one's judgment narrower and narrower until it vanishes completely. A master of the spirit is then dead to his mission. He can no longer discern or guide. He is a corpse and can corrupt as he is corrupt. At times it is alluring to descend, it is almost always tempting, because at the bottom there are sensual satisfactions. We also are going down to the valley to find rest and food. But if that is necessary to our bodies, it is not necessary to satisfy sensual lust and spiritual sensualism. You are allowed to reach one valley only: the valley of humility. Because God Himself descends into it to abduct humble spirits and raise them to Himself. He who humbles himself will be exalted. Any other valley is lethal, because it removes one from Heaven."

Vol. 8, p. 338

"Because that is what souls are in need of, a guide who may lead them to the Life, to the Truth, to the right Way. God is merciful towards the souls that seek and do not find, not through their fault, but because of the laziness of shepherds who are like idols. God is merciful towards the souls that get lost when they are abandoned to themselves and are received by Lucifer's ministers, who are always ready to welcome those who have lost their way, to make them proselytes of their doctrines."

Vol. 9, p. 223

"There is always time to make amends for laziness and sins committed so far, there is always time while man is on the Earth and has days in front of him during which he can redress wrongs done – those will be with me in my Kingdom."

Diligence means you are enthusiastic about what is in front of you. You will apply a spark of excitement and energy to whatever task is in front of you. Enthusiasm comes from the word "en" meaning within and "theos" meaning God. So having God within is where the word enthusiasm comes from. With God's energy moving through you there will be no resistance and no avoidance of work or effort. You will move through things without thinking too far ahead and since your mind will be focused on the task in the moment, you will not be distracted and more energy and power will move through your concentration. You will not put things off or wait to do things on some special break in your schedule, you will do things as soon as you possibly can. Most of your hard projects that you make such a big deal about could be divided up in small increments that could be done a little each day and by the time you have that imagined window of opportunity, like Sunday afternoon, to do that project, you could have most of it done or all done before that nostalgic day arrives. That is love and enthusiasm and diligent effort.

IDLENESS

Poem Vol. 1, p. 237

"In that house they love work, and they would love it even if there was plenty money, because the working man obeys the command of God and frees himself from vice, which like tenacious ivy clenches and suffocates idle people, who are like immovable rocks. Food is good, rest is serene, hearts are happy, when you have worked well and you enjoy the resting time between one job and the next one. Neither in the houses nor in the minds of those who love work can many-sided vice rise. And in its absence, love, esteem, reciprocal respect prospers and tender children grow in a pure atmosphere and they thus become the origin of future holy families."

Vol. 3, p. 134

"Woe to you, rich and fast living people. Because it is among you that the greatest impurity thrives and idleness and money are its bed and pillow. You are now sated. The food of concupiscence reaches your throats and chokes you. But you will be hungry. And your hunger will be terrible, insatiable and unappeasable forever and ever. You are now rich. How much good you could do with your wealth? Instead you do so much harm both to yourselves and to other people. But you will experience a dreadful poverty on a day that will have no end. You now laugh. You think you are triumphing. But your tears will fill the ponds of Gehenna. And they will never cease."

Vol. 5, p. 69

Marjiam asks Jesus, In that case why did you work so hurriedly as to get blisters on your hands? Jesus says, "I got them because I no longer work with my hands. See, my dear child, how painful idleness is? Always. When one resumes working one suffers twice as much because one becomes too delicate. Now, if it hurts one's hands so much, how much will it hurt one's soul? See? This evening I had to ask you to help me, because my hands were so sore that I could not hold the rasp, whereas only two years ago I could work for fourteen hours without feeling any pain. The same happens to those whose fervor and will become loose. One becomes too flaccid and feeble and grows weary of everything very easily, as the poisons of spiritual diseases affect those who are weak. On the other hand, it is twice as difficult to do good actions, which previously, when one was always in practice, cost no effort. Oh! It never pays to be idle saying: "After this period of time I will resume working with fresh energy!" One would never succeed, or would succeed with the greatest difficulty." Marjiam asks: "But you have never been idle." "No. I have done other work. But you can see that the idleness of my hands has been detrimental to them. And Jesus shows his hands which are red and blistered. Marjiam kisses them saying, "My mother used to do that to me when I hurt myself, because love heals." "Yes, love heals many things."

Vol. 3, p. 331
"God is Self-sufficient and takes care of everything in creation. I have just told you that God is present also in the buzzing of a mosquito. He does not get bored, does not worry. He is not a poor man, the master of an immense empire in which he feels he is hated and lives trembling with fear. He is Love and lives loving. His life is continuous Love. He is Self-sufficient because He is infinite and most powerful, He is Perfection. So numerous are the things created that live because of His continuous will, that He has no time to grow weary. Tedium is the fruit of idleness and vice. In the Heaven of the True God there is neither idleness nor vice."

Vol. 4, p. 316
"I tell you solemnly that idleness is sin. But it is better to be idle than accomplish wicked deeds. And I also tell you that it is better to be silent than speak idly and wickedly. Even if to be silent is to be idle, do that rather than sin with your tongues. I assure you that on Doomsday justification will be requested for every word spoken idly to men, and that men will be justified by the words they have spoken, and by their words they will be condemned. Be careful, therefore, because

you speak many words that are more than idle, as they are not only idle but also harmful, and are spoken to drive hearts away from the Truth speaking to you."

Vol 5, p 97

"The exaggerated and fearful anxiety of a selfish person is different from the prudent care of a just person. It is sinful to be avaricious for the future, which perhaps, we shall never see. But it is not sinful to be thrifty to secure a piece of bread, also for one's relatives, when there is a shortage. The selfish care of one's body is sinful, when a person demands that all those around him should worry about him, and avoids all work or sacrifice lest his body should suffer, but it is not sinful to preserve it from wasteful diseases, the result of imprudent behavior, which diseases are a burden for relatives and a loss of profitable work for ourselves. Life is given by God. It is a gift of His. Consequently we must make a holy use of it, without being imprudent or selfish. "

Vol. 5, p. 48

"Consider the case the Pharisees charged you. They stated that you were unclean because you were taking food to your mouths with dusty, sweaty hands, that is, with unclean hands. But where did that food go? From your mouths into your stomachs, from your stomachs into your intestines and from your intestines into the sewer. Can it thus make your whole body unclean, and what is contained in your body, if it only goes through the passage destined to fulfill the task of nourishing the flesh, and the flesh only, and then ending in a sewer, as it is right it should? That is not what makes man unclean. What makes man unclean is what is entirely and exclusively his own, procreated and brought forth by his ego. That is, what he has in his heart, and from his heart rises to his lips and to his head, corrupting his thoughts and words and making him wholly unclean. From the heart come evil incentives to all actions. And if the heart is wicked, they will be as wicked as the heart. All actions: from idolatry to insincere grumbling... All these wicked things, which from

88

inside come outside, make man unclean, not eating without washing one's hands. The Science of God is not a base thing, mud upon which any foot can tread. It is something sublime, which lives among stars, from which it descends with rays of light to perfect the just. Do not, at least you, tear it from Heaven to disgrace it in mud."

Vol. 5, p. 76

"The original sin will be cancelled in those who believe in Me. But their souls will still have an inclination to sin, which they would not have had, had there been no original sin. It is therefore necessary to continuously watch and take care of one's soul, as a solicitous mother does with her little son, who has been left weak by an infantile disease. So you must not be idle, but always active to grow stronger in virtue. If one falls into sluggishness or tepidity, one will be more easily seduced by Satan. And each grave sin, which is like a serious relapse, will always predispose one to diseases and spiritual death. But if Grace, restored by Redemption, is assisted by an active indefatigable will, it will remain. Holiness and Grace. Which are safe wings to fly to God."

Vol. 8, p. 246

"I have noticed that where Jesus is, one is never idle. He is the first to teach the beauty of manual work, when other evangelical work is interrupted."

Vol. 9, p. 11

"You must be able to tell the difference between an idle word and a useful one. A word is idle, and sin generally flourishes in idleness, when one speaks of other people's faults with someone who can do nothing about them. Then it is plainly lack of charity, even if what one says is true. As it is lack of charity to reproach someone more or less sharply without giving advice at the same time."

GREED versus SELF-CONTROL

Greed is defined as excessive desire to acquire or possess more than what one deserves or needs. It comes from the etymological root 'gher" which means to "want." The synonym for greed is avarice meaning 'eager' or 'extremely desirous.' A second definition for 'greed' means to want to eat or drink more than one can reasonably consume; gluttonous. Gluttony, which is a form of greed, means excess in eating or drinking. It is indulging in something, such as an activity, to excess: It means to be voracious (insatiable appetite for food, a pursuit or an activity); and ravenous, which means extremely hungry, predatory and rapacious.

You can see the similarity between greed and gluttony in that both contain an excessive desire for something; money, food, power, or any other pursuit or activity. You can crave food or money and they have a similar result. In both cases, you will be corrupted by your own immoderate desire and misplaced value on something material to fix an internal need. The internal need is for connection and love. In the case of food, the nurturing energy and supply as a child was interrupted and frustrated which caused you to take over the nurturing yourself. Since you did not really know how to nurture yourself like your parents should have, you started to do it angrily and reactively without really knowing how to do it. So you picked sweet foods or foods that turn quickly into sugars in the body. Since these are less satisfying and nutritious in the long run, you started an addictive process of not being able to stop the cycle of emotional hunger. You will not be satisfied and so will eat more gluttonously to compensate for the emptiness of not having received nurturing parenting.

When you are seriously overweight, which means over 25 pounds overweight, then you have been compensating for maternal love with food. You need to stop. You need to control yourself and cut it out. Any negative emotion, like the kind that drives an eating disorder will soon have a demon supporting that pattern until it becomes a full blown condition.

GLUTTONY
Vol. 1, p. 179
Mary says: "I defeated gluttony, both of knowledge and of enjoyment, by agreeing to know only what God wanted me to know, without asking myself of Him more than what I was told. I believed unquestioningly. I overcame the innate personal delight of enjoyment because I denied myself every sensual pleasure. I confined the flesh, the instrument of Satan, together with Satan, under my heel and made of them a step to rise towards Heaven. Heaven! My aim. Where God was. My only hunger. A hunger which is not gluttony, but a necessity blessed by God, who wants us to crave for Him. I defeated lust, which is gluttony carried to the extreme of greed. Because every unrestrained vice leads to a bigger one. And Eve's gluttony, which was already blameworthy, led her to lust. It was no longer enough for her to enjoy pleasure by herself. She wanted to take her crime to a refined intensity and thus she became acquainted with lust and was a mistress of lust for her companion."

Vol. 1, p. 237
"In that house there is frugality and it would be there even if there was plenty of money. They eat to live. They do not eat to satisfy their gluttony, with the insatiability of gluttons and the whims of epicures who fill themselves to the extent of being sick and squander fortunes on expensive food, without giving one thought to those who are without or with little food, without considering that if they were moderate, many people could be relieved of the pangs of hunger.

Vol. 1, p. 303

Jesus says, "The two most common means adopted by Satan to conquer souls are sensuality and gluttony. He always starts from material things. Once he has dismantled and subdued the material side, he attacks the spiritual part. First the morals: thoughts with their pride and greed; then the spirit, obliterating not only its love, which no longer exists when man replaces divine love with other human loves; but also the fear of God. Then man surrenders his body and soul to Satan, only for the sake of enjoying what he wants, and enjoying it more and more. You saw how I behaved. Silence and prayer. Because if Satan performs his work of a seducer and comes round us, we must put up with the situation without any foolish impatience or cowardly fears. We must react with resolution to his presence, and with prayer to his allurements. It is useless to debate Satan. He would win, because he is strong in his dialectics. Only God can beat him. And so you must have recourse to God that God may speak for you, through you. You must show Satan that Name and that Sign, not so much written on paper or engraved in wood, but written and engraved in your hearts. My Name, My sign. You should answer back to Satan, using the word of God, only when he insinuates that he is like God. He cannot bear that. Then after the struggle, there comes victory and the angels serve and defend the winner from Satan's hatred. They restore him with celestial dews, with the Grace that they pour with full hands into the heart of the faithful son or daughter, with a blessing that caresses his soul."

Vol. 10, p. 197

"And in my Head, My eyes, My mouth, My nose, My tongue, each had their torture. To make amends for your glances, so anxious to see what is evil and so forgetful of seeking God, to redress the too many, too false, filthy and lustful words that you utter, instead of using your lips to pray, to teach, to console. My nose and My tongue suffered their tortures to make amends for your gluttony and your sensuality of olfaction, through which you incur imperfections, which are

the ground of graver sins, and you commit sins through the eagerness for superfluous food, without taking pity on those who are hungry, food which you can afford very often by having recourse to unlawful means of profit."

When you are overly invested in accumulating wealth and material possessions you have created an idol. That wealth may be to augment your self-esteem, but that is a lie, because your self-esteem is not improved by wealth, but by a relationship with God. Real love improves and augments self-esteem. Greed wants wealth, money, power and position. It is a fire that craves and so unless God blesses your desires, you will find they make you feel sick and nauseous.

Vol. 1, p. 107
"And Eve understood. Now Malice was inside her and was gnawing at her intestines. She saw with new eyes and heard with new ears the habits and voices of beasts. And she craved for them with an insane greed."

Vol. 2, p. 113
"What is necessary then to gain Paradise and rest on the Father's bosom? It is necessary not to be greedy for wealth. That is, not to be eager by wanting wealth at all costs, even by going against honesty and love. Not to be eager to such an extent as to love the wealth one possesses more than Heaven and one's neighbor, refusing to assist a needy neighbor. Not to be greedy for what wealth can offer, that is: women, pleasures, a bountiful table, magnificent garments, which are an insult to those who are cold and hungry. There is a currency that can change the unjust money of the world into a currency having legal tender in the Kingdom of Heaven. And that is the holy wisdom in turning into eternal riches, the human riches which are often unjust or the cause of injustice. That is, you must earn honestly, give back what you obtained unfairly, make use of your riches with parsimony and detachment, learning how to become detached from them,

because sooner or later they will leave us, whereas good deeds will never leave us. You must consider that."

Vol. 2, p. 360
"Greed. 'He has what I have not got. I want what he has. But only by disparaging him I can obtain his position. And I am going to do it. Will I be lying? What does it matter? Will I be stealing? What does it matter? Will I ruin a whole family? What does it matter?" Of the many questions that the shrewd liar asks himself, he forgets, he wants to forget one question. This one: "And if I should be found out?" He does not ask himself such question, because a prey to pride and greed, he is like one whose eyes are closed. He does not see the danger. He is also like a drunk man. He is intoxicated with a satanic wine and does not consider that God is stronger than Satan and takes vengeance of the calumniated man. The liar has given himself to falsehood and foolishly relies on its protection."

Vol. 3, p. 484
"You, who for the sake of gold, sin more or less lightly, or more or less gravely, and the more you sin, the more you laugh at what your mothers and teachers taught you, namely, that there is a reward or a punishment for actions done during life, will you not consider that because of that sin you will lose God's protection, eternal life and joy, and you will have in your hearts remorse and malediction, while fear will be your companion, fear of human punishment, which is nothing when compared to the fear which you should have but you have not, of divine punishment. Will you not consider that you may have a dreadful end because of your misdeeds, if you have gone as far as being criminals; and an even more dreadful end, because it will be an everlasting one, if for the sake of gold, your misdeeds have not gone as far as shedding blood, but have despised the law of love and of respect of your neighbor, by denying assistance to those who are starving through your avarice, or stealing positions or money or defrauding by means of false weights, through your greed?

No, you do not consider all that. You say: "It's all an idle story. And I have crushed such idle stories under the weight of my gold. And they no longer exist."

Vol. 2, p. 283
"And you will work miracles. But as long as there is too much flesh in you, you will not work them. It is of no use. By flesh I mean the corrupted passions, the triple craving and the train of vices that follow the treacherous triple craving... Like the children of a filthy bigamous union, the pride of the mind gives birth, through the greed for flesh and power, to all the evil that is in man and in the world..... No, I am not asking for your material death. I want animality and Satanism to die in you, and they do not die as long as the flesh is satisfied and falsehood, pride, anger, arrogance, gluttony, avarice and sloth are in you."

Vol. 3 p. 92
"If the sacrifice of a goat or a lamb and the offer of a few coins were prescribed, the reason is that every evil is founded on two roots: greed and pride. Greed is punished through the expense for the purchase of the offering, pride by the open confession of the rite: 'I am making this sacrifice because I have sinned.'"

Vol. 4, p. 61
"Lust, sensuality, greed for money raise their voices to criticize good deeds. Good people do not criticize. Never. They understand."

Vol. 5, p. 317
"He who is incredulous, has not a righteous soul" says the Prophet and his word condemns those who provoked and insulted Me. I do not condemn them. But the Prophet, who foresaw Me and believed in Me, condemns them. As he describes Me, the Triumpher, so he describes a proud man, saying that he is not honorable, as he opened his soul to greed and insatiability, as hell is greedy and insatiable. And

he threatens, "Trouble is coming to the man who amasses goods that are not his and loads himself with think mud." Evil deeds against the Son of Man are that mud, and the desire to deprive Him of His holiness so that it may not dim one's own, is greed."

Vol. 9, p. 15
"And always remember to judge with the same method also those who commit the sin of greed for other people's riches or property. Because if it is a cursed sin to be greedy without need and without pity, robbing the poor, and acting against justice harassing citizens, servants, or peoples, the sin of him who steals some bread to appease the hunger of his children and his own, after his neighbors refused to give him some, is by far less grave."

Vol. 1, p. 179
Mary says: "I defeated the avarice of the First Parents renouncing my Creature before the time. A mother never renounces her creature unless she is forced to. Whether her heart is asked to renounce her creature by her country or by the love of a spouse or even by God himself, she will resent or struggle against the separation. It is natural. A son grows in our womb and the tie that links him to us can never be completely broken. Even if the umbilical cord is cut, there is a nerve that always remains: it departs from the mother's heart and is grafted into the son's heart: it is a spiritual nerve, more lively and sensitive than a physical one. And a mother feels it stretching even to exceedingly severe pangs id the love of God or of a creature or the need of the country take her son away from her. And it breaks, tearing her heart, if death snatches her son from her. And I renounced my Son from the very moment I had Him. I gave Him to God. I gave Him to you. I deprived myself of the fruit of my womb to make amends for Eve's theft of God's fruit.

Vol. 4, p. 387

"One of you asked Me: 'How will I cure in Your Name.' Always cure the spirit first. Promise the sick people the Kingdom of God if they can believe in Me, and once you have ascertained their faith, order the disease to depart and it will go away. And do likewise with those whose souls are ill. Stimulate their faith first of all. By means of sound words inspire them with hope. I will then come to grant them Divine Charity, as I put it into your hearts after you believe in Me and hoped for Mercy. And be not afraid of men or of demons. They will not hurt you. The only things you are to fear are: sensuality, pride and avarice. Through them you would hand yourselves over to Satan and devilish men, who also exist."

The virtue that heals greed and avarice is generosity. Generosity means the willingness to give and to share. It means to be kind and give freely. The simple test of whether what you are doing is designed to get you something or to actually give something is all it takes to determine whether you are generous or not. If most of what you do is calculated to make sure you are taken care of, then you are not generous or kind. If you are noble in character and magnanimous in your love for people, then you are generous. To hoard things for yourself, to calculate when you are going to get something for you, to manipulate and orchestrate situations to your benefit is greedy and selfish.

Vol. 5, p. 497

"But why be avaricious with good God who is so generous with you? Why do you expect only to be saved, and with some difficulty, and you do not wish to attain great holiness, which gives eternal peace at once? Come on, be generous with your soul."

The virtue that heals greed and gluttony is moderation and self-control. Self-control means to control your emotions, desires and actions by your own will. It also means to hold in restraint or to check. If you want to learn self-control start with small things like: 1. remove the expression "um" or "like" from your vocabulary. 2. Remind yourself to sit up straight. 3. Spend two weeks avoiding alcohol or 4. Spend 30 days avoiding sex or any thought of sensuality.

One way to evaluate your level of self-control is to ask yourself these questions: 1. How often do I push the snooze alarm in getting up? 2. When you try to control your emotions, people still know what you are feeling. 3. People say you have no patience. 4. When you feel tired you don't exercise or work out. 5. At a party, how often to do you regret some of the things you said? 6. Do you have a problem controlling your urges, like drinking, sex or gambling? 7. How often do you act on the first impulse you have? 8. Do your friends tell you that you are bad with money and unable to manage your finances? If you have a few of these, then you need to bolster up your self-control muscle and discipline yourself.

Vol. 7, p. 252
"Be sober in all your dispositions, because moderation is proof of moral strength,..."

CHARITY VERSUS ENVY/JEALOUSY

Envy, covetousness, jealousy and begrudging are all the same thing. Envy/jealousy is defined as a feeling of discontent and resentment aroused by a desire for the possessions of another. It means to wish for longingly. Covet is defined as to feel a blameworthy desire for what is another person's. It is to feel a painful or resentful desire for another person's advantages. The etymology of the word "envy" is 'to see' or 'to look.' Remember, Eve saw what she could have after the serpent tempted her.

To envy is to expect that the blessings someone else has should be yours. Did you earn the right to have them? Would not God give you those things if you were ready for them? If you desired a person's wealth or situation or partner, why don't you prepare yourself for those things and ask God to grant you them when you are prepared. But to want what is someone else's is to sin against God's love. God takes care of all creatures. When we do not trust God enough to take care of us and we want what we are not ready for. If you are ready for something, then God will give it to you. Please prepare yourself to be worthy of the blessings you desire. What someone else is experiencing might happen to you if God wills it, or if you have prayed for it and God grants it to you. But there are a whole lot of negative feelings inside of jealousy and envy that makes you think bad thoughts about what someone else is experiencing. It is such an easy step to think negatively about someone else who receives benefits in their life? Why are you not loving towards your sister or brother for the gifts they receive honoring God for taking care of people with such wisdom? If you are filled with selfishness, then you would not feel that others should get anything at all.

You are the only one worthy. You are the only one that deserves benefits and gifts. You, of all people, deserve to be blessed better than anyone else. That is ridiculous if you examine yourself with a righteous retrospection of all the things you have done that were mean and self-centered. You do not actually deserve anything really, so why do you get yourself so puffed up? Only one is good, that is God.

Vol. 4, p. 487
"Oh! You are blessed if coming from farther away you will go beyond those who belonged to the house of the Lord and went out of it, urged by the ten commandments of Satan: dislike of God, love of oneself, corruption of cult, harshness towards parents, murderous desire, attempt to steal other people's holiness, fornication with Satan, false witness, envy of the nature and mission of the Word, and the horrible sin which ferments and matures in the depth of hearts, of too many hearts."

Vol. 5, p. 48
"From the heart come evil intentions, murder, adultery, fornication, theft, false witness, blasphemy. From the heart come avarice, lust, pride, envy, wrath, immoderate desires and sinful idleness. From the heart come incentives to all actions. And if the heart is wicked, they will be as wicked as the heart. All actions: from idolatry to insincere grumbling... all these wicked things, which from the inside come outside, make man unclean, not eating without washing one's hands."

Vol. 2, p. 286
"It is said: "You shall adore nothing but your true, one, eternal God." It is said: "I am a strong jealous God."
"... Jealous. Of what? Of which jealousy? Of the petty jealousy of petty men? No. the holy jealousy of God for His children. The just, loving jealousy. He created you. He loves you. He wants you. He knows what is harmful to you. He is aware of what is capable of separating you from Him. And He is jealous of what interposes between the Father and His

children and diverts them from the only love which is health and peace: God. Understand that jealousy which is not mean, is not cruel, is not restrictive of freedom. It is infinite love, infinite goodness, unlimited freedom, which gives Itself to the limited creature, to draw to Itself and in Itself for ever, and associate it to Its infinity."

Vol. 2, p. 364

"Envy! What is to covet other people's property but avarice and envy? My dear children, envy separates man from God and unites him to Satan. Do you not remember that Lucifer was the first one to covet what did not belong to him? He was the most beautiful of the archangels and enjoyed the vision of God. He should have been happy with that. He envied God, wanted to be god and became a demon. The first demon. Another instance: Adam and Eve had been given everything, they enjoyed the earthly paradise and God's friendship, blessed with the gifts of grace which God had granted to them. They should have been satisfied with that. They envied God's knowledge of good and evil and were driven out of Eden and became disliked by God. The first sinners. A third instance: Cain envied Abel's friendship with the Lord. And he became the first killer."

Vol. 6, p. 354

"Jealousy! What can you think of more slanderous for a wife than jealousy? And what is a clearer indication of the state of the heart than jealousy?"

Charity is the antidote for jealousy. Charity is defined as, 1. compassion, giving, sympathy without prejudice; friendship for its own sake. 2. Love directed first toward God but also toward oneself and one's neighbor. 3. benevolence or generosity towards others; forbearance or indulgence in judging others. It comes from the Latin, 'caritas' meaning affection. A synonym for charity is mercy.

103

Charity is thinking good thoughts and feeling good feelings for other people. There is no bitter longing in charity. There is no sad, forlorn feeling of lack and being passed over in charity. Charity suffers for the one you love and makes sacrifice for those you care about. It does not close its heart off hoping for a balancing out of the blessings that another has received, waiting for God to make it right. This is jealousy that poisons where there should be celebration.

CHARITY

Vol. 1, p. 137
Mary says, "The first charity towards our neighbors is to be exerted towards our neighbors. This must not seem a pun to you. There is charity towards God and charity towards our neighbors. Charity towards our neighbors comprises also charity towards ourselves. But if we love ourselves more than our neighbors, we are no longer charitable, we are selfish. Also in lawful matters, we must be so holy as to always give priority to the needs of our neighbor. Be sure, my children that God provides for the generous by means of His power and His bounty." "... That is why I worked for Elizabeth, postponing my own work. I was not afraid that I would not have time. God is the master of time. He provides for those who hope in Him, also in normal things. Selfishness does not speed matters up, it delays them. Charity does not delay, it speeds up. Always bear that in mind."

Vol. 1, p. 161
"A charity that knows how to forgive, that wants to forgive, and forgive in advance excusing wholeheartedly the imperfections of our neighbors. It is necessary to forgive immediately, accepting every extenuating circumstance."

Vol. 1, p. 375
"Every time you are charitable, God will grant you the grace of abundance."

Vol.3, p. 78

"Those who have been most unmindful of themselves, have given the most. It is difficult to be unmindful of oneself. Man is made of recollections and the ones that raise their voice most are the memories of one's ego. You must distinguish between ego and ego. There is the spiritual ego (Self) or the soul that remembers God and its origin from God, and there is the inferior ego of the flesh that remembers its passions and the numberless exigencies concerning its whole being. They are so many voices as to form a choir, and unless the spirit is quite strong, they overcome the solitary voice of the spirit that remembers its nobility as child of God. It is therefore necessary – with the exception of this holy memory that should always be stimulated and kept green and bright – it is necessary to learn how to forget yourselves, in all the memories, the needs, the timid reflections of the human ego, in order to be perfect disciples."

Vol. 3, p. 115

"Keep the good you may do free from the violating sensation of the world, keep it immune from human praise. Do not profane the scented rose of your charity and of your good deeds, as it is a true censer of perfumes agreeable to the Lord. Good is profaned by a proud spirit, by the desire to be noted when doing good and by the quest for praise. The rose of charity is then dribbled and eaten away by the big slimy snails of satisfied pride and the censer is filled with the fetid straw of the litter on which the proud man basks like a well fed animal. Oh! Those deeds of charity accomplished to be pointed out by people! It would be better, much better, if they had not been performed at all. Who does not do them, commits a sin of harshness. Who does them letting people know both the amount given and the name of the person to whom it was given, and begging for praise, commits a sin of pride by making the offer known, and commits a sin of spiritual avarice as he wants to store up human praises... It is straw, nothing but straw. Let God and His angels praise you."

Vol. 3, p. 140
"Charity is an absolution. Be charitable to everybody and in everything. If God gives you much assistance to keep you good, do not be proud of it. But endeavor to climb the full length of the ladder of perfection and give a hand to those who are tired or unaware and to those who are easily disappointed. Why do you observe diligently the splinter in your brother's eye if first you do not go to the trouble of taking the plank out of your own eye?"

Vol. 3, p. 401
"They do live in the Temple and the smoke of the lamps, that is of honors, blackens them, but no light descends upon them: and all passions nestle in them like birds and cats, while the fire of their mission does not give them the mystical torture of being burnt by the fire of God. They are refractory to Love. The fire of charity does not inflame them, as charity does not clothe them with its golden brightness. The charity of double form and double source:

Charity of God and of neighbor, the form; charity from God and from man, the source. Because God withdraws from a man who does not love, and thus the former source ceases; and man withdraws from a wicked man, and also the latter source ceases. Charity deprives a loveless man of everything. They allow themselves to be bought at a cursed price, and to be led where it suits profit and power."

Vol. 3, p. 450
"He who loves his neighbor and practices charity both towards his family and his subjects, and extends it to unhappy people, has already Religion in himself."

Vol. 3, p. 460
"Rudeness is always against charity."

Vol. 4, p.45

"And after the promise of forgiveness Wisdom speaks saying what is legal and what is not legal, and it reproaches and shakes, not out of harshness, but out of maternal anxiety to save. How often your hardness becomes more impenetrable and unyielding to Charity bending over you. How often you run away while Charity speaks to you. How often you scorn it. How often you hate it. If Charity dealt with you as you deal with it, woe to your souls. Instead, see, it is the untiring walker who comes looking for you. And it reaches you even if you hide in the darkest of dens."

Vol. 4, p. 221

"A holy life, mildness, purity, charity and humility will never be lacking in the wise and little voices of God. They will always be lacking in the others."

Vol. 4, p. 304

"Charity does not consist only in giving alms or comforting by means of words. Charity is accomplished through charity alone. Do not think that this is a pun. I had no money and words were not sufficient for this case. There were seven people on the threshold of starvation and anguish. Despair was already putting forth its black claws to grasp and strangle. The world was withdrawing harshly and selfishly before this misfortune. The world was proving that it had not understood the words of the Master. The Master evangelized through deeds. I was capable and free to do it. And it was my duty, on behalf of the whole world, to love those poor wretches whom the world did not love. That is what I did."

Vol. 4, p. 434

"Mother tell me, since you are so wise. If I throw out innuendos against someone, or worse still, if I utter slander about someone, I obviously commit a sin. But if I laugh at something, at an event, which is known to everybody, something which makes people laugh, for instance, if we remember the surprise, the embarrassment and excuses of a liar when he was found out and we laugh again as we did in the past, is that still wrong?

It is an imperfection against Charity. It is not a sin like backbiting, or slander or innuendo, but it is still lack of charity. It is like a thread pulled out of a piece of cloth. It does not tear or wear the cloth out, but it affects the firmness and beauty of the fabric and makes it subject to tears and holes. Do you not think so? Peter rubs his forehead and feeling rather humiliated he replies: *'I do. I had never thought of that.'*

Think about it now and do not do it anymore. Laughter may be more offensive to charity than slaps in the face. Has someone made a mistake? We have found someone guilty of lying or of other faults? So? Why remember it? Why remind other people? Let us cover with a veil the faults of our brother, saying: 'If I were the culprit, would I like another person to remember my fault or remind other people of it?' There are people who blush in their heart, Simon, and suffer so much because of it. Do not shake your head. I know what you want to say. But, believe me, also guilty people may blush thus. You must always think: 'Would I like that done to me?' you will then see that you will no longer sin against charity. And you will always have so much peace in your heart."

Vol. 5, p. 28

"It is the first commandment: Love and Love. He who does not love lies in professing to be Christian. It is useless to frequent the Sacraments and rites, it is useless to pray if one lacks charity. They become formulae and even sacrilege."

Vol. 5, p. 202

"They will be gathered in my Name. No longer Romans or Libyans, Greeks or people from the Black Sea area, Iberians or Gauls, Egyptians or Hebrews, but souls of Christ. And woe betide those who will distinguish souls, whom I equally loved and for whom I equally suffered, according to their nationalities. He who should do that would prove that he has not understood Charity, which is universal."

Vol. 6, p. 80

"And humility is the clearest sign of my doctrine. Those who want to follow me must love Truth, Purity and Humility, they must be charitable to everybody and heroic in defying the opinion of men and the violence of tyrants."

Vol. 6, p.91

"What has the Master done and what has he made you do and practice today? Charity in its multiform ways. Charity towards God. Not just the charity of vocal ritual prayer. But active charity which renews you in the Lord, despoiling you of the spirit of the world and of the heresies of heathenism, which is to be found not only in heathens, but also in Israel, in the many customary practices that have replaced the true holy Religion, as open and simple as all things coming from God. Not good deeds, or apparently good to be praised by men, but holy deeds to deserve the praise of God."

Vol. 6, p. 157

"Do you know how man can possess infinite love? By being so united to God, as to be all one with God. Then, as the creature disappears in the Creator, it is the Creator who really acts, and He is infinite. And My apostle must be like that, all one *with their God through the power of love, which is so close to the Origin as to dissolve in it. It is not the way in which you speak, but the way in which you love, that will convert hearts. Will you find sinners? Love them. Will you suffer because of disciples who go astray? Try to save them through love."*

Vol. 6, p. 426
"Never be without charity toward your neighbor. Was he born a poor wretch? Love him because he endures great pain. Did he become unhappy through his own fault? Love him because his fault has already become a punishment. Is she the parent of a wretch born such or who became such? Love him because there is no deeper sorrow that the grief of a parent struck in his child. Is it a mother who has given birth to a monster? Love her because she is literally crushed by such grief, which she considers the most inhuman."

Vol. 7, p. 64
"Be ready to fight the fire then. And what is that fight? A stronger and stronger Faith, a firm will to belong to God. It means to belong to a holy Fire. Because fire does not consume fire. Now, if you are fire of love for the true God, the fire of hatred against God will not be able to harm you. The Fire of Love defeats every other fire. My doctrine is love and those who accept it enter the Fire of Charity and cannot be tortured by the fire of the Demon."

Vol. 7, p. 82
"God is joined to Charity. And Charity is truly and more intimately and really the spirit of His Spirit even than is a married couple who love each other deeply. God Himself is Charity. Charity is but the most manifest and illustrative aspect of God. Of all His attributes Charity is the sovereign and original one, because all the other attributes of God originate from Charity. What is power but active Charity? What is Wisdom but teaching Charity? What is Mercy but forgiving Charity? What is justice but ruling Charity? And I could go on thus with regard to all the numberless attributes

of God. Now, after what I have said, can you believe that he, who has no Charity, has God? No, he has not. Can you imagine that he may accept God, but not Charity? There is one Charity only and it embraces Creator and creatures and it is not possible to have only one half of it: that for the Creator, without having also the other half: that for our neighbor.

".... After the end of the world no other virtue will survive except Charity, that is, the Union of all the creatures who lived in justice, with the Creator."

Vol. 7, p. 134
"I solemnly tell you that true charity, faith and hope are tested more in sorrow than in joy, because the excess of joy is often the ruin of a spirit not yet perfected."

Vol. 7, p. 156
"You must therefore have kind hearts, because God is love and He prescribes love, because the Law is love, because the prophets and the Books of Wisdom advise love and My doctrine is a doctrine of love for your neighbor and particularly for the poor and needy, to whom you can give all forms of love by means of bread, beds, clothes, comfort and doctrine, leading them to God."

Vol. 7, p. 364
"When one is full of love one cannot have any other desire or science but love."

Vol. 8, p. 505
"It is sufficient to have charity, which is the spiritual lyre with paradisiac notes. When a soul lives in charity, its heart is calm and it can hear and understand the voice of God."

Vol. 9, p. 413
"They say that there is no blood or love superior to the Temple, and they thus teach people not to love their neighbor. I tell you that above the Temple there is love. The

law of God is love and he, who does not take pity on his neighbor, does not love."

Vol. 9, p. 510
"What I was able to do, I did it because I was all one with the Love. Also when the God-Love withdrew from me, I was able to be love, because I had lived of love during my thirty-three years. It is not possible to reach perfection, as is required to forgive and put up with our offender, if one has not acquired the habit of love. I had acquired it, and I was able to forgive and bear that masterpiece of an Offender, which was Judas."

Vol. 10, p. 448
"You will not have the Kingdom of God in you, if you do not have love. Because the Kingdom of God is the Love, and appears with the Love, and through the Love it is established in your hearts in the brightness of a huge light, that penetrates and fecundates, removes ignorance and gives wisdom, devours man and creates the god, the son of God, my brother, the king of the throne that God has prepared for those who give themselves to God, in order to have God, God, God alone. So be pure and holy through fervent prayer that sanctifies man, because it plunges him into God's fire which is Charity."

YOU ARE LOVED

You are loved by God or you would not exist. God keeps you in consciousness and wanted you to be a conscious part of God when God placed himself within you. The spiritual path is only necessary because as human beings, we have strayed off course and become somewhat unrecognizable to God from the way God pictured us when we started out. We have distorted our nature and covered over our beings with useless things and messed up thinking to the point that we lost consciousness of who we are and what our real nature is. God sent Jesus and Mary to show us by living example what a human being is like if there is no distortion or negative emotions and thinking to cloud our real nature. The spiritual path is the way back into our natural state of being. We are Christs in the making and God walking around in flesh bodies. It is not presumption to say that we are God in the making. Jesus said, "Know you not that you are gods?" We are made in the spiritual image of God and so our nature is the same.

God wanted you to have the same freedom to shine, to live and to love that God has and so you are equipped to be as creative and emanating as God. The one thing you are never to do is to presume yourself to be greater than God. That is dangerous pride and will be seen by God as jealousy and corrupt. You are corrupt if you try to be greater than you are, greater than God. In the process of your training, you are overwhelmed at times by how far you have to go to become like the teacher or the real priests. You are amazed at how many times you have to struggle to change anything in yourself even to overcome one single thing in your character. Your habits can be so strong and entrenched that you have to exert heroic effort just to budge that problem or fault just a little. You try to overcome a bad habit in yourself and it just beats you into the ground and humiliates you with how difficult it is to change. When you try to change yourself by your own efforts, you find it is like pushing a large boulder up a steep hill. You try and the boulder rolls back over your foot or your leg. You try again and again and then think sad thoughts about the spiritual path or you get angry at your teacher for being exempt from all of the hard and overwhelming tasks of mortal life. This may come as a surprise to many of you, but the teacher when they first entered the spiritual path was as wounded and beat up on the road of life as you are and sometimes much more beaten up than you. Then out of compassion your teacher asks you if you have asked Jesus or Mary for help with your problem. You sheepishly mention that "no" you forgot to ask them. If you try to do these changes yourself, you will fall short because your attempt to change yourself implies that you want to take personal credit for the improvement. That is your pride wanting to make sure it was because of you that you succeeded. You succeeded all by yourself. If you leave God out of the picture, you will have something in the end which God will not recognize and which will not have the light and love of God present in the outcome. Please ask God, Jesus and Mary for help no matter how easy you think something is going to be, so that you inoculate yourself against the yeast of pride that might suggest to you that you can do things alone. You cannot breathe without God's help, so let that fantasy go. You are not anything except what God created you to be. Your purpose is to express the being and nature of God. God's nature is light, life and love. So if you express anything besides this, you are expressing something else besides God. If you express something besides God, then you will separate yourself more and more from God's presence and love. That will be very unfortunate because you cannot be happy without a relationship with God.

In every case of a person appearing to be happy, just wait a few minutes and you will find that person in deep depression. Or they get angry and impatient. It is absolutely impossible to be truly and genuinely happy unless you have a relationship with God. To leave out the one who created you is essential stupidity. You did not build yourself from some architectural plan. You were not the engineer that made your vascular system and your heart beat. That took a much higher intelligence than a human being. If some of you still wonder if a random set of cells just organized your system in such a beautiful fashion, then realize that those abilities and capabilities that you have were thought up by someone. And it is an amazing body that we have. God did that. Without being the way God made you, you cannot be at peace or even in contentment. If you do not acknowledge your Creator, you cut yourself off from the personal relationship with God. That would be sad because there are so many benefits to being in a conscious relationship with the Father. If you know the being who created you, then you can conform your thinking and feeling to the nature of that being. When you do that, you will start to regenerate and move closer into oneness and love with God. All created beings have an obligation to be grateful to the one that created them and to be zealous in learning who the being is that thought them up. That is humility and intelligence. If you look to God for the prototype of what God's nature is, then you can become more and more like God since that is the highest good any creature can express. You cannot express more perfection than God. You can only strive to be as good and as clear as God. That is the highest good. You will never be better than God. You will never encompass God because the created cannot ever completely encompass the Creator. As Jesus said, "I and my Father are one." We can be one with God, but not better than God.

What is blinding and humiliating to you at times is that you have to let go of things in order to attain a new consciousness. You cannot hold on to everything you have accumulated if you are striving to experience God. You have to make room inside yourself for God. That involves a very humbling experience of shedding your pride and discarding your fears so that you have room inside for God to enter. God is deep inside you already, but you might only suspect that. You do not know that yet. Your head might firmly believe that God is the center of you and everything. But you have to clear out your concepts and bad habits to make sure the body, mind and emotions are in the right relationship to God to really be able to experience God in God's fullness and purity. God will not enter into your body, mind, and emotions unless those areas have been sufficiently purged of old habits, negative energy and pridefully held concepts. This letting go that we talk about is a form of death. The teacher encourages and watches you to see if you care enough about God that you will let go of anything that is not of God. They ask you to let things die in you so that God can have room to move into your body, mind and emotional house. You have to make room. You cannot expect God to compete with some of your special interests because God will not try to convince anyone that God is important. You have to come up with that wish all by yourself. God will not prove to you that having a relationship with God is important. You should already know that and have that as the most important striving of your whole life. It is the first commandment, by the way. You shall love God with all of your heart, your mind, your soul and your strength. It was our density that caused God to lay these commandments down as codes of living. We were too dense to realize that God created us and deserves the best fruits of our labors and the first love of our hearts and minds.

As you start to get it that you have to change in order to receive the consciousness of God, you understand that you are being asked to enter into your death process. You have to die to all of the things that you formerly valued as important except God. God is the source of all, so God has to be the most important thing in your life. In our fast-paced life, so many things get to be so important. We have a relationship and that takes all of our time and is so intense, exciting and absorbing. Then the children come along and they are everything to us and since they take so much of our focus, it looks like all of our effort and time is about them. Then there is school and work and career building. Another huge amount of effort and focus is required to get ahead in the world and get to a place that you can see your way out of debt. In all of this whirlwind of activity, God takes a back seat and is embroidery for walls and curtains on the structure of your life. Your sadness and creeping depression crawls forward on the lines of your face and the aches in your bones. You begin to see the futility of the material life and the endless tasks, and bills and responsibilities. What is the meaning of this life? Why did I come here? What am I really supposed to be doing here? If you are wise, you will take the time to ask those questions and get down to what is real inside you. The answers always come for those who really want to know. A path always opens up for the one with the courage to discover the real meaning of life. The call from your soul goes into the mind of God and God sends you to the people who can introduce you to the path that will be right for you and the teacher that will take you to God. God's love is so strong, that God draws all people back to God through love and attraction. God is the only game in town that satisfies and heals the soul. Everything else robs you of your divinity and makes you much less than you were created to be. Aren't you sick of your life as you have known it? Don't you yearn for a time when your soul can say "I am in peace now because I know God's love." Let that time be now.

BLINDED BY THE LIGHT

The winter of the soul comes to everyone at some time in their life. In winter, the life force pulls back and stores up for the essential task of survival and persistence in time and in life. Our life as souls has a similar cycle of pulling back to assess our successes and our failures. We evaluate our comings and goings and the meaning of our existence in the light of something deeper than worldly standards of success. If we are honest and if we have a true desire to know, then we will come to the realization that our life so far has been a series of catastrophes and accidents that have tossed us around and possibly bumped some sense into us. It is difficult to determine at times whether the experiences we have gone through have deepened us or made us angrier and sadder. But one thing brings us to alertness and honesty: we are a far cry from where we would like to be. We have not moved very close to the real goals of life, to feel the love inside our hearts. We don't know that much for sure and we are still groping around in a dark closet too far from the door to grasp where we are or how to get released.

I know that some of you feel really good about where you are and how you are growing. Some of you know that you could be much more than you have expressed so far in consciousness, in peace or in love. You are in one of two camps: either you are dismayed that you have so much to learn and so many things to change about yourself, or you feel disturbed when the teacher points things out to you that are still a problem for you and you need to fix those and change them. Here you are again creating your own agenda of wanting to feel okay and being hurt or upset that the teacher sees more that you should change about yourself to be closer to God. OR you feel so bad about yourself already, you can't stand to have anyone add more pain to the your already over-burdened self-concept. In this case, the teacher's hands are tied. They are restrained from burdening you more by telling you what you have to work on or they are supposed to be encouraging and supportive of where you are applauding your celebration of how many changes you have already made in your life and how much better things are.

What we typically do is stretch you a little regardless because that is our job. We see your next step and we see the ones you have made. We do encourage you and applaud your successes and your overcoming yourself. It is hard to change and the teacher knows firsthand how difficult the path is because they travelled it before you. They were not exempt from any stage of the path and it was not easy for them and it will not be easy for you. The easy things don't stretch you, do they? I know that you are beating yourself up, some of you. So I would rather be the one who corrects you because you do it viciously or meanly and I won't do that. We will understand you and also be firm with you when you are acting out and trying to get everyone around you to fall into line and recreate with you your family dynamics. We will most especially not cooperate with you when you are trying to make your role in our spiritual family the same as you had when you were in your dysfunctional one. We are not a dysfunctional family. We are dedicated to not have those power plays and abusive energies in this order. We have to be about love and light. Love joins people together and light shows up everything and clarifies motives and intentions. Light is what makes it possible to understand and know things because the Light is intelligent and penetrating in its nature. It moves into the core of things and shows them up for what they are. You can't see unless you have light. You cannot know what is really going on inside another person unless you have Light and unless you care enough to love them. Our order and this spiritual school is all about love and light. That makes this whole spiritual body an alive organism that can be the vehicle for the Christ to move on this planet. This spiritual vehicle will be the way that people will be able to experience God, experience light and love.

Since we are dedicated to express light and love, we are not afraid of what the world or other people might think about us. We all know the flack that we get for being who we are and how we are. The world thinks we are crazy for not indulging our sensual side. The world thinks we are scary because we do not hold back from seeing what is going on with people and stating what their motives are. We are not afraid which by itself would be enough for the world to call us many names. There are no scandals in our order and we are dedicated to keeping it that way. There are no sexual relationships happening with our ministers and those they teach. There are no power struggles among the leaders of our spiritual school. Most orders are taken down by those two things because the leaders have not fully transformed and become like God created them to be. When you do not allow the light and love inside you to transform those areas that formerly acted as renegades to God's way, you will act out on your subordinates at some point and make a living hell of your well-intentioned spiritual group. That has happened so many times. It will not happen here. We accept donations and expect people who value our teachings and way of life to tithe just like in the churches. We will accept your generous gifts and we appreciate them greatly.

We are a new spiritual family, much like Jesus and Mary created when last they were here. Jesus and Mary are our new parents for the spiritual age that is upon us. We can become like them and eventually each of you can have Jesus and Mary as your elder brother and sister. But first you must be so filled with Light and so completely changed in your thinking and in your heart that your life starts to be like theirs. Your heart has to beat with theirs like one heart-beat. You have to have their mind, their perspective, their sight and their energy inside you in order to be close to them. You cannot just spout religious jargon and beliefs and hope to be known by them. They are not cheap in their relating. Something trivial and cheap is not going to draw them close to anyone. They demand sincerity, honesty and integrity in every part of your life. They cannot be fooled and will take you at your word. Do not toy with them as they are the sovereigns of this planetary evolution of human beings. Don't fear them either because they are the most loving and intensely conscious beings you will ever know. Invite them into your heart and let them come in to see where you are and how you have been doing. Invite them in and let them know you and start to help you. You cannot do this yourself. If you fear them, they will not come in. If you fear them, then you think they will take something from you or hurt you in some way. They will never hurt you, but they have to be able to come in and say and do whatever it is that their nature does. Light shows things up and heal things. Love opens you and draws you closer. Love breaks your heart from all the anger, pain and sadness that has tortured you these lifetimes. Let them do what they are masters of. They are masters of life and love and human beings. Give yourself over to them. When you do, you will be blinded by the light and it will love you more than you have ever known.

YOU DON'T HAVE ANY PROBLEMS

You need to start thinking of yourself the way God thinks of you or you will never get better. The way you were created is the way you are. You were given everything you could possibly need and everything that you want, in truth. What you really need is love. Love was placed in you in the beginning and the blueprint for how to live, create, propagate, work and learn was inside you as well. Everything the new created being would need to grow and gain from experience was given to us. Immediately we forgot our Father and felt separated and lost. In this empty place of separation and distance from God's close love, we fell into doubt about our existence and the meaning of life. We began to listen to false voices and suggestions of how to comfort ourselves and soon we were far away from God. God continued to inspire and try to get our attention and give us whatever help we might notice or accept. But mostly we slipped away and fell into a sort of animal survival existence. We began to think of ourselves as opposed to the needs of everyone else. We became selfish, proud, stubborn and willful.

Lifetimes of struggle and pain have convinced us further that it is every person for themselves. What you can eke out of existence is due to your resourcefulness and cleverness. The most fit and most cunning get the top positions in society. It is better to look good than to feel good. You work on the appearances, you manipulate information to suit your needs. In other words, you claw and lie your way to a position of power and unassailability over other people. You don't love. You fear and compete and work all the angles to be better than other people. In this endeavor, human beings are only excelled by demons. We have become a proud people with thick necks and stubborn minds. We have sold our birthright for a few crumbs of recognition. This is the state of most human beings on the earth. They can't love because they are scared to death that someone will get something they don't have. They don't love because it is all about getting and taking.

All the problems that attend such a disaster can be categorized and inventoried. There are the numerous health problems. There are psychological problems of anxiety, depression, compulsions and withdrawals. There are the full demon possessions in schizophrenia and psychosis. There are the emotional troubles of insecurity, self-hatred, addictions and acting out the anger on oneself and others. Then there is the implosive disturbances of phobias, obsessions and other traumas suffered at the hands of parents who were also troubled. Numerous manifestations of a multitude of problems suffered by human beings are evident in most people. From these observations come the simple-minded statements that "Everyone has problems;" "Nobody is perfect;" "Just you wait, you'll get yours;" "It could happen to anyone." Each of these statements might actually be thoughtful under certain circumstances, but they ignore a fact of life: that people choose their conditions in life. They may not know how they made a decision that produced a certain result, but they definitely have the power to make decisions. Everything what happens to a person has been the result of choosing. Either you chose to be in a situation where something might happen, or you actually thought and felt the kind of thoughts that produced that result in your life. Most people do not see the cause/effect relationship, but that does not change the outcome. Nothing can happen unless it is created in mind. Sometimes a person can be so out of touch with themselves that they are not aware of what kinds of feelings, thoughts and actions were building in them to produce a particular result. But this does not change the facts that they chose the experience.

Everything affects everything else. A little emotion here, an acceptance there and a thought over here and another conclusion and a series of causes are sent out in the universe to produce a specific result. Just because you don't remember what all the pieces are does not mean it will be less effective. People get sick sometimes. That happens. If you arrive somehow in Tulsa, Oklahoma, we are not particularly interested in how you got there. Maybe when we have time or are bored we might ask you that. But you are in Tulsa, so what are you going to do about it? What decisions do you have to make now to make the most of it or to change the situation? That is how you should treat sickness. Do something to fix it, change it or accept it. Stop doing the things that caused it or become consciousness of what you are ignoring so it doesn't happen again. Learn from your experiences. When you feel alone and sad, you can do the same thing. You can assess where you are and determine how you would like to feel. Then make the decisions necessary to change your situation, your feelings, into what you want them to be. This may take work, since sometimes you have to change some pretty serious things in yourself in order to feel different.

Most people are mad. They want to make a few important people pay for their condition and so they are still little and small and weak and self-pitying. They are not grow ups yet. A grown up takes responsibility for their condition and just makes decisions and steps out in constructive ways to change things They don't add tears to their spilled milk. They don't get others to commiserate with them for how hard everything has been. Two little babies often will gravitate to one another to nurse each other's wounds. But they do not grow strong that way. They lean on one another until a wind blows them both over. Life has a way of sorting these things out and resolving matters with truth in mind. The truth is neither of them is strong and so both will fall or one will fight with the other for dominance. The whole foundation of their relationship is wrong and it will all come out in the wash. A grown up says this: "I am where I brought myself. I am fully responsible for it. I don't particularly like where I am. I will change it. I know it is up to me. No one else is to blame. I need to rely on God and myself to get me out of this. If anyone helps me it will be a great blessing, but I have to take some pretty major steps on my own to fix this." A child whines: "No one will help me. I hate myself. Why doesn't someone come and rescue me from my condition? If those people would have just done this or that, I wouldn't be in the predicament I am in now. What is wrong with those people that they don't see me? Etc." This is a whiner, someone who is not ready to take any responsibility for their own life and make things happen to change their situation. We have worked with mad people and they make everyone else mad around them. They are not about to do any real work on themselves as they want everyone else to pay for their frustrations. We find out which of these you are in fairly short order. In our order, you cannot be a baby unless you never want to be counted on and never want to be empowered to serve. That is a choice. But also, we won't expect anything from you either because you have informed us that you won't help until you are coddled and nurtured again like a little baby. A baby cannot be disciple of Jesus and Mary. A disciple has to take orders. A disciple has to learn to love, help and forget about themselves. You see how important it is for you to be self-supporting, self-motivated and responsible?

You have only the problems you created. You don't really have any problems that are real. God made you and you are no different than that perfect pattern that God envisioned when you were formed. Yes, I know. You have covered over your true nature with so much slime and mud that you are barely recognizable to God. You are all sin for the most part. I know you seem innocent as you feign childishness. As you desire to harken back to a time when you should have been coddled and loved. But you weren't coddled or loved well for some good reason. You were not loved the best way

126

because you did not deserve that as a child. You were learning how it feels to be treated the way you treated others in the past. I know you have all heard me say that. Yet, you don't change yourself very much. You don't take your bull by the horn and train yourself to give and love and serve and forget about you. You need to squeeze the bull out of you so that you are clean and empty and pure for God.

You don't have any problems. None of your problems are real. They are a fig leaf of your imagination. They cover your pride in thinking you are better than you are. You are only as good as God made you and that has nothing to do with you. But you can be an aberration if you like. You have a right to distort yourself, but there is karma to pay for that. You can dream up problems and try to get unseeing people to believe that you have them. But you cannot fool a real priest or teacher. They know you have only the problems you are on life support with. You run that silly intravenous line of a problem into your vein thinking you will get you some strokes, some comfort, some relief for it. You do it to get out of some work or responsibility and then you pack people around you that believe it is important for you to be on that intravenous lifeline. Then you have a cushy little group of blind friends who don't see what you are doing. You are trying to make people pay for you and carry you. Anyone who does not support your regime, you discard like an old pair of shoes. Some of you are so nice about it. Some of you are so subtle and unassuming, and yet that is exactly what you do. You don't have any real problems. God did not make you with problems and does not see problems in you. Of course, you have been trying to convince God and everybody of your difficulties. But God is not buying it. Your teachers will not buy it. In truth you do not have any problems. The only problem you have is trying to make sure you have one. That is a huge problem. But that is not real either.

How different your life would be if you were done with your troubles. You would be able to help. To serve and love and pray and bring people close to God would be your aim and desire. Nothing would get in the way of this striving and you would have a very full life. You don't see Jesus or Mother Mary thinking about themselves and how much they have to give, do you? You don't see Jesus have a bad day and being insecure about his abilities or worrying about whether people like him. He did not stop one thing he was set out to do and did not stray from his mission to redeem. He was confident in what God gave him to do. He was faithful and knew that God would provide because God had blessed his mission. You can have such faith and trust in God if you would just find out what you are supposed to do and then proceed to do it without allowing yourself any indulgent distractions. Let God take care of giving you benefits and graces for the work you do and the love you give. Let God clear your path and remove your obstacles. Trust the process of clearing the old patterns out of your being and scraping off the mud from your heart, mind and body so that you can be like you were created. The path is a path of return. It is not going to some place unknown. Your soul knows the place and that place is in the radiance of the love of God. There is nothing new about it. It is as old as God. It is as fresh as the morning and there is healing in its wings.

LONELINESS

Everyone has experienced loneliness. Maybe it was one intense time of loneliness or the loneliness lasted for years, but it is a universal human experience. Aloneness and loneliness are very similar. Aloneness means no one is by your side or on your team. Loneliness is more existential, meaning underlying and pervasive, a state of how you seem to be existing. You have most likely heard that we come into the world alone and die alone. People speak in such exaggerated one liners and expect everyone to squeeze their experience into that. The saying sounds impactful and powerful and so we want to go along with it as if it is true. But we actually spend quite a number of months inside the consciousness and energy of our mothers in order to make the passage into this world. Then since we are extremely helpless, we can't be left alone for even a minute without parents fearing the worst. So we don't arrive alone. We can and do die alone because death sneaks up or arrives late or comes at an inopportune time, unplanned and surprising. Often our soul chooses to be alone during the passage out of earthly existence as it is less traumatic when relatives aren't wailing and screaming.

Loneliness is a little different. It comes when we notice people not paying much attention to us when we are young. We experienced long periods of time where no one knew what we were doing and did not seem to be concerned about where we were or what was happening to us. We thought about that, formed conclusions about ourselves, like we are not good enough, and then had feelings about that and started to feel lonely. At first we would express a forlorn look or a shutdown sadness that would be advertised and wafted out like an odor into the house or wherever some important person might notice. When almost no response was obtained, gradually over time, we assumed we were alone. Then we acted sad, afraid or angry about that. But the lonely feeling continued and did not abate.

You noticed extended periods when no one was around and began to amuse yourself. When you looked up and there was still nobody there, you wondered about it. Then you felt a little scared that it might have something to do with you not being worthwhile or maybe you were bad and did not understand how you were bad. The next step is that you formed a conclusion in your mind that important people did not care about you and you felt hurt and sad. If that situation was not remedied, then you felt lonely and you accepted that nothing will change. When people are lonely they do many interesting things. They self-comfort in pretty terrible ways. They secretly hate themselves and stop caring how they act or who they are hurting. They let themselves go physically, emotionally and spiritually. They hang out with people who are also wounded and lonely and who don't care what effect their actions have on other people. All the strange behaviors human beings demonstrate are due to this feeling of reaction to loneliness.

The loneliness became familiar and customary. Exciting events, challenging situations and interactions with people interrupted the loneliness at various points in the week, but the underlying experience of being unseen and alone did not go away. When a caregiver paid attention to you and really spent a lot of time with you listening and understanding you, you were relieved and lifted from this malaise of loneliness for a few hours. Then each time after getting your hopes up that the loneliness would not have to be experienced again, you would be left alone and sink back in to the emptiness and sadness of being alone. This experience is all too familiar to almost everyone on this planet. We came here focused on our parents and helpless to take care of ourselves. We needed our caregivers for every single thing in order to survive. We focused completely on their comings and goings to the point that everything they did and did not do became life itself to us. Is it any wonder that since they were inconsistent and not quite perfect, that our experience would be abandonment and loneliness? That is the state of most people.

The sad part of this history of our lifetimes is that over and over again we have both neglected others and karmically have been neglected by people. The cycle continues until someone breaks the pattern. We treat people a particular way and then we suffer at the hands of others who give us that exact same treatment. We get what we put out. We look outside ourselves for love and attention. We never get the love and attention we want, so in our desperate need for love we look to squeeze love out of the people around us. That frenzy of emptiness makes us not able to really see the people around us and so when we are needed by the ones who are dependent on us, we are checked out and unavailable. Our children don't get us because we are desperately clawing to steal whatever crumbs of love are lying around. So the cycle goes on and on. We are lonely and angry and we pass this condition on to our children and they are supposed to get over it and grow past it. The whole pattern of looking outside ourselves for love and attention is grafted into us and we run the squirrel cage of the loneliness pattern for lifetimes.

You can be lonely because you don't have a partner or you can be lonely because you do have one. You can make others take care of you and then be incredibly lonely. Or you can play the hero and take care of everyone and be completely alone without anyone to take care of you. You can use your children to make you feel better or have them comfort you when you get sad. Then the whole family will feel alone because the kids see that mom or dad cannot be an adult with the confidence and stability to be strong. The parents feel like imposters pretending to be wise when really they are a little boy or girl wanting someone to be strong for them and take care of their needs. You will definitely be lonely when you look to another human being to take care of you. If you ask the God within that person to take care of you, that works fine because you are acknowledging that you need God. But to forget God and just look to the actual human in front of you, you will be lonely.

I don't know about you, but this pattern seems ridiculous and without any lasting value. Loneliness attracts lonely people and other vacuous people into your life who are as insatiable for love as you are and then you hack out your misery on each other until one of you waffles and decides to be the slave of the other, cowering before the threats and manipulations by giving in and doing what the stronger tyrant demands. Loneliness grows into a gaping trench of disconnection. Most of you found the path in such a state and are hardly aware of how mad you are about this interior lack of love and attention. You can distract yourself with work and be incredibly busy. That way you don't have to face the aloneness or feel your feelings. You might try various activities to keep your spirits up, or even imbibe real spirits to bolster your mood. Any addiction will do when your life is empty. Then it hardy matters what you do because you only jump from one sensation to another voraciously looking for anything to keep you from feeling the insatiable loneliness of being distant from God.

The solution to loneliness is looking within. Inside you, the real love you have been looking for awaits. God told me that the reason for loneliness is turning away from God and looking to the world for love. Looking for people to love you is much the same as looking to the world, unless you find someone who is connected to the source within and loves other people from that place. When you love from the source within, you are standing in for God and giving people the love that moves through you. Love wells up in the person connected. Love overflows when you are hooked into to God and have allowed the gentle streams of God's healing energy to line you up again to the reality of perfect love. Even when you come into the presence of such a being, you are suspicious and reluctant to allow yourself to relax and let their love, which comes from God, flow into you. You expect the same treatment as the important ones in your life gave you. You expect the fountain of imperfect love to suddenly and unexpectedly stop. So you brace, demand and whine to let everyone know you expect the worst or at least the same as before. The teacher is patient with you because they were the same as you on their way to developing trust and openness. They understand since they were there where you are now before they turned within for connection to the source of love. They know what it takes to not feel lonely any more. They know the courage one has to have to leave all the false loves that only bite your intestines with a fire of craving that cannot be satisfied. They know the process of leaving things that are false for things that are true. They know if you only have a little taste of good love, that you will be changed and healed. Then you will grow into heroes of love because you will have put away your suspicions and your mistrust. You will open and loneliness will drain off of you like a downpour washes over a highway.

As you wake up from your anger and hurt at not being seen and loved, you will accept God's love into your being and not worry if a person is able to love you or not. It won't matter to you anymore because you will have in your heart all the good feelings and attention from God that you could conceive of and you will have tasted of Heaven. It is that easy. But you have to let go of being mad. You have to leave the pattern of looking outside for relief from your loneliness and pain. Step within and feel the powerful reality of what you have been missing. Open to the love and loneliness will become a page of your history that can be left as a record of what you used to know.

Even if you are hated or criticized, you won't feel alone or afraid because you have the love inside you.

Vol 3, p 387

"Sorrow is a cross, but it is also a wing. Mourning divests to reclothe. Rise, you who are weeping. Open your eyes, get rid of nightmares, of darkness, of selfishness. Look. The world is the barren land where one weeps and dies. And the world shouts: "help" through the mouths of orphans, of sick, lonely, doubtful people, through the mouths of those who are made prisoners of hatred by treason or cruelty. Go among those who are shouting. Forget yourselves among those who are forgotten. Recover your health among those who are sick. Be hopeful among those who are despairing. The world is open to those willing to serve God in their neighbor and to gain Heaven: to be united to God and those whom we mourn. The gymnasium is here."

LOSING YOUR LIFE

It would be sad if you lost your life. It would devastating if you died without having the chance to do all the things you wanted to do or learn everything you wanted to learn. Wouldn't it be really sad if your life was shortened by an accident or catastrophe which you had no control over and could not anticipate? We often don't appreciate the challenges of our lives and do not take very good advantage of our opportunities. So it is a common experience for people to be surprised about events that seem out of their control. Each day we have opportunities to be kind, to be conscious, to stand up for truth, to represent peace and we don't. We have this habit of putting off our perfection and responsibility until later. Our responsibility is our ability to respond – response-ability. We are able to respond, but do we feel the impulse to respond when we can? Often we put things off until tomorrow as today has too many worries and challenges for us to contend with. If we had extended sight like the eye of the eagle and could see for fifty miles ahead, we could see how important today's decision will be for our future. We could see how just a small bit of effort today would tip the scales in someone's favor or provide sufficient grace to bring a blessing to someone who was faltering and wavering between two minds, two decisions. Our efforts would make it possible for another person to overcome some difficulty that they would not be able to overcome without our help. They may not know you at all, but you contributed to their overcoming and succeeding just by your good effort and good attitude.

When you put things off that are hard, you are setting grace aside for some future time when you will be open for its benefits. When you don't take advantage of an opportunity to stretch, give or grow, you are tormenting yourself with staying the same and keeping the status quo. Essentially, you are staying the same because it appears easier. You don't want change because the familiar is more comfortable than the adventure of launching into the unfamiliar. The more tight-gripped you are on how things are now, the more death and tumultuous change is at your door. Life moves on, so when you try to keep things steady and the same, life pushes up against that stuck door. It will blow that house down since it was founded on fear, on sand. When you heat sand, you get the most brittle and fragile substance –glass. Glass is a brittle protection against the weather, but at least you can see out of it. When you are stuck, you will see life from behind glass and anything hard could shatter your world. The more you try to not change, the more fragile you become. You don't want to lose your life as you know it and you clutch on hard to that steering wheel hoping to keep from driving into a ditch. But the harder you clutch, the more life seems to elude you. Life becomes sullen and sad as you squeeze yourself more and more into a tight little package. Constriction and narrowness are the result of such decisions. The Spirit can't move through you and your life cannot receive any blessings. Blessings widen your sight, clear obstacles out of your path, open the doors and windows for fresh air and make your body and mind alive again.

The sadness of losing your life is your experience so far. You have lost so much life because of your own decisions and fears. Your anger has also contributed in a major way to your shut down energies. You are vigilant around everyone because they might treat you the way someone else did and you have a fight or flight response to anything that looks or sounds the same. Your whole existence seems wrapped in a challenge to the world to defy your history and startle you into proving that they are safe for you. If people have to prove to you that they are safe, they get tired of your petty tests and let you stew in your own juices. You get to have it your way.

Pushing people away is another result of feeling that you have no life. You shove people away refusing to let them in to care about you. You see them the same as other important people and make them pay for what those other people did to you or did not do for you. If you push people away, you are pushing God away. God is inside those people and inside of you. If you reject people, you are actually resenting and rejecting God. At the very least, you are rejecting the good in that person and not seeing properly. As you shut down more, shoving aside possible connections with people, you are losing more and more life and opportunities to express life.

Actually, the way out of this mess is counter-intuitive. Jesus said, "If you seek to save your life, you will lose your life. If you lose your life, for my sake, you will save it." Jesus is saying if you try to preserve and keep your life the way you have it, you will lose it. If you clutch on to the meager existence you have and the short-term gains you have achieved, you will lose it. Because the holding on implies a lack of faith and trust in God. You are in fear of things getting worse. That is a kind of prayer. Or you are satisfied with where you have come and how you have achieved. This creates a prideful stagnation that rests on your laurels and luxuriates in your short-sighted contentment. How far have you come, really? How advanced are you spiritually? One of the priests that left recently said that they did not feel that they should be taught forever and had had enough teaching. They felt they had grown enough and had made some positive changes and did not feel the teacher-student relationship should go on indefinitely. Well, I was thinking that that was one of the most ignorant things I have heard in a long time because I can't imagine ever being so together that Jesus and Mary can't teach me a thing or seven. I can only imagine that God has an infinite number of lessons and expansions for me that I haven't even conceived of and unless I am in a learning relationship with God, I would miss out terribly on that experience. So that was truly ridiculous and I hope none of you ever get that ridiculous to make a statement like that in the future. We will always and eternally be learning, growing and being taught by beings far in advance of where we are. That should be comforting and a great love and grace that God provides for us.

If you think you are all set, then you will lose even what you think you have, as Jesus explained. So don't ever get satisfied with where you are because that could spell a downward tumble. Be grateful for all the blessings you receive but don't get lazy and comfortable and imagine that you know it all or have every bit of experience on the subject because that will cut you off from your Creator.

How much of what you call 'life' is yours? Did you create life and think yourself into being? No? Well, then why do you claim sole possession of everything and pretend that the life you are living is yours? When did everything get to be about you? It's my time. I did that. It's my choice; it's my creativity, it's my man; it's my woman; it's my talent; it's my intelligence; it's my love. None of the good things are created by you. All of the goodness in you is from God, on loan to you for your use. But you have to know where it comes from or you will lose it. All the qualities, talents, graces and gifts that you have were given to you by God and are part of God's arsenal of gifts bestowed on human beings for their use. When you forget your place in creation, you imagine all those were developed by you and you want the personal credit for all of them. Then you have fallen off the wagon or you soon will fall off the wagon of grace. Conversely, all of the faults, imperfections, negativity and ugliness and meanness are developed by you. You own them. God does not have anything to do with those and so you may humbly take credit for every one of those because you manipulated God's energy and distorted the life energy into those mis-creations of negativity. You can take credit for anything dark, evil or nasty, weird, wasteful and wicked. Those are yours.

138

The Law of God is very precise. There is a quote from somewhere, "The mills of the Gods grind exceedingly fine." This means the law of Cause and Effect is perfect and you will account very meticulously for what you put out. If your action and thought is self-serving and self-aggrandizing, then you will reap accordingly. You will receive the reward of our efforts. If everything is about you, you will get the acclaim you want, but it will not really be satisfying. It will not fulfill you because you thought only of yourselves and so any rewards will fall to you alone. The acclaim can only come from circumstances and people since you have conveniently left God out of the picture. God will not be part of it since you gave God no credit and did not ask God's help. God withdraws from the proud, the pompastic.

Vol. 4, p. 405

Jesus in explaining the words "He who has will be given much and he who has not, even the little he has will be taken away." "And that is right. He who has and works with what he has, will be given more and even in excess. But he who has nothing, because he did not want anything, will be deprived also of what was given to him. With regard to the useless servant who betrayed my confidence and left inactive the gifts I had given him, throw him out of my property and let him go and weep and eat his heart out."

The Law says if you have, then you will receive more. If you love and give, the gifts come to you because you have established the pattern of giving and God's energy and love must of necessity flow through you and bring more blessings. If you try to control that, you squeeze it down and limit it immensely. But if you don't have much already, then you have an ongoing pattern of not moving much energy, not giving much of yourself and generally being selfish, that you have put out so little, hardly anything can come back to you. You have been the unfaithful servant who took the talent that his master had given to him and went out of fear of the strictness of the master, buried it in the field so as not to lose it. Then when his master came back, the servant returned the original talent intact. The master took that talent away from him because of his selfishness, fear and from not making any good use of it, and gave it to the one who made great use of the one talent the master gave him. Jesus is teaching an important truth here. If you are selfish, you are going to close down the pipeline from God and get less and less and less because you are not trusting that all good things come from God and that your job is to just let those gifts pour through you to other people and into creation. If you hold onto them or control the energy, you will shut yourself off from God. If you fear that you will have less if you give of yourself, then you never tried it or you would know what a beautiful gift God gave us to be able to love and give of ourselves. That opens the flood gates of love and vitality flowing through us more powerfully than anything we can think of.

In your best interest, I am asking you to lose your life. I want you to give of yourself to God and to people so much that you stop thinking about yourself and just let the love, light, energy and spirit move to whomever and wherever. That will be losing your life. Then you will start having immense energy and love moving through you. The greatest clue you will need in this process is to forget about the results. Don't look for the results of your giving, your movement of energy. That is actually not your business. God will take care of that. Just keep giving and loving and leave the results to God. If you look to the results, you have to sit down on the park bench and speculate how well you have been doing and that is selfishness once again. Also, while you are assessing how you are doing, you stopped giving and are just dreaming of the past or the future. Nothing is happening while you are doing that and you are giving yourself a little break. Why don't you stop doing that because that stops your spiritual growth? Give and give and don't look back.

Vol. 8, p. 137

"The same happens to those who descend spiritually instead of ascending. One's virtue and wisdom become more and more limited and one's judgment narrower and narrower until it vanishes completely. A master of the spirit is then dead to his mission. He can no longer discern or guide. He is a corpse and can corrupt as he is corrupt. At times it is alluring to descend, it is almost always tempting, because at the bottom there are sensual satisfactions. We also are going down to the valley to find rest and food. But if that is necessary to our bodies, it is not necessary to satisfy sensual lust and spiritual sensualism. You are allowed to reach one valley only: the valley of humility. Because God Himself descends into it to abduct humble spirits and raise them to Himself. He who humbles himself will be exalted. Any other valley is lethal, because it removes one from Heaven."

Vol. 3, p. 387

"Every good deed is the origin of great things, which you do not even imagine. And the effort man makes against his own selfishness can cause such a wave of love, capable of rising higher and higher, supporting in its limpidity him who caused it, until it lifts him to the feet of the altar, to the heart of God."

Vol. 1, p. 138

Mary says: "God is the master of time. He provides for those who hope in Him, also in normal things. Selfishness does not speed matters up, it delays them. Charity does not delay, it speeds up. Always bear that in mind."

LEARNING IS CONTINUOUS

God has many lessons for us, even after we think we are done with our lessons. God is our Father and has outlined our course of development over eons of time and experience. We are on an immense journey that has no end and will last eternally. We co-exist with God after our initial creation. We are immortal beings even if we do not act like it. Our immortality is a divine inheritance given out of love, but that does not mean we know what that is or what is required to be faithful to that.

It is a great mistake to think that this one short lifetime is all you have. It is selfish to assume that enjoyment is the only purpose to life. Enjoyments become sour after indulgence. Pleasures strip the body of sensitivity after satiation. Immoderate emotions or bodily attention makes humans dense and sluggish. In this one life, we have tremendous opportunities to grow, learn and be useful. Remember, God has a plan for each of us. God has in mind the whole future of our evolution into full co-creators, like God. That is the plan. It is inconceivable to most animal-humans at this stage of development. How does a co-creator function and feel. What kinds of thoughts travel in their minds? What does a co-creator feel inside? God is perfectly patient and knows how long created beings take to learn things. It looks from our observation that it takes people well-nigh forever to learn most of the important things in life. Lessons have to be gone over and over in order to only slightly make a dent in the consciousness. That is the nature of this level of development called earth.

Some pundit described our present development as further along than the Buddha in an article I read recently. It went on to say that Buddha did not go that far into enlightenment compared to what is possible today. In some ways, that sounded prideful and stupid as if the speaker slipped into the body and mind of Buddha and spoke for him. It is safe to say that the Buddha had a powerful experience that completely changed the history of the world. We know of Buddha from the teachings that he passed down and the descriptions, however poor, of what he experienced in mediation. As with any great Avatar teacher, their disciples add description to his teaching in an effort to explain what Buddha taught. These descriptions, just like in the case of the Jews adding commentary to the teachings of Moses, make for a hodge-podge of confusing restrictions that choke the life out of the original message. Christianity is replete with such confusing additions to Jesus' teachings and it has caused a bad symphony of misconceptions. There is one point that makes sense and that is that the possibility of spiritual consciousness now is greater than in the past. The density of the people back in Buddha's or Jesus' time was much different than today. Some people have grown more sensitive over the last 2500 years. It is sad that it is only a few people have evolved sufficiently to be able to say that the level of their spirituality is higher than the level of the original disciples of Jesus when they first met Jesus. If we have been incarnating many times since Jesus and Mother Mary were on earth, then hopefully some of those souls grew spiritually and evolved to a new level of consciousness. Unfortunately, most people have not even arrived close to where Jesus and Mary were when they walked on the planet. Most people are primitive and barely awake. Most do not feel God or have any inkling of God and do not think much about it. But beware of the prideful mind that thinks our advanced society and technological prowess exempts us from the simple teachings of Jesus or Buddha in terms of coming into oneness with God. The teachings are eternal and cannot be improved by intellectualisms.

144

God knows how difficult human beings are. God sees our struggles and density and provides lessons of Karma for us so that we can take our lessons on the level we are able. God's love makes each soul a unique class in itself and God watches over the perfection of the lessons given. It is insanely slow in most cases. God has to watch a human soul block learning a lesson over and over again and God still has a perfectly positive attitude about how hard that needs to be for that dense a person. When the soul has mastered the difficulty and overcome it, a new lesson is given. Millions of lessons are stored up in God's mind waiting for the right moment to be given. Lifetimes and lifetimes of lessons that are needed to mold the soul and bring it back to the original whiteness and blessed state when it was created. Our mistakes and stubbornness took us so far away from God and we are responsible to drag ourselves back into God's compassion and healing. We cannot be healed unless we humble ourselves and implore God to take us back and help us. We are not able to do anything by ourselves and so must seek the help of God, who wants to help. God created us and wants to support our development and help us with our lessons.

I look at our students and sometimes those learning to be ministers and I see sluggishness and dejection. I feel the sadness that you have in trying to overcome a difficulty or a problem. I can see how much you want to be free of the old pains and misguided opinions of the past. I can understand how the hurts from the past have crushed your spirit and stomped on your heart to make you not want to give and not feel strong enough to overcome yourselves. Ask for help and it will be given to you. Pray to God, Jesus and Mary to come to your aid and lift you up out of your condition. Ask them to teach you how to think and behave so that the negative patterns are broken once and for all. Be consistent. Consistency is your saving grace as it keeps a new pattern going until it becomes an automatic part of your nature. In a month's time, a new pattern will obliterate the old pattern until it seems like that old style of behaving was so far in the past, it will seem like another lifetime. That is a sign that you are really changing and growing. When the past feels old and historical, then you are growing.

The slowness and lethargy that I feel from some of the students is the resistance of the old patterns holding on and the new pattern not quite alive as yet. When a rocket is launched, the first stage of burning fuel is just to get enough lift to start to get off the ground. A tremendous amount of fuel is needed to get the rocket, which is usually millions of pounds, to even budge off the launch pad. 90% of the fuel is used just to get up out of the earth's atmosphere and that is 90% of the weight. The actual module that is being launched is roughly 1% of the weight of the whole rocket. Learning something new is like the launch of a rocket. It takes a great deal of effort to change something in you and make it stick. It can be done because people are doing just that every day. Most of you are give-up artists and get discouraged extremely easily. You seem to accept any suggestion of defeat and fall down at the slightest obstacle to progress. Why are you so mushy? Why do you look for any chance to give up? It seems that you do not want to succeed, the way some of you carry on. Many of you are fits-and-starts learners. You make a strong push toward growth and then you sit down in the middle of the path and mope over the slightest set-back. You use anything as a set-back and reason to take a small mental vacation from consciousness. After all, who can be expected to keep up an effort in the face of so discouraging a life and so many unsupportive people? You rationalize your failures and give way too much credit to yourself for you successes. When you succeed and get blessed with something, you immediately take credit for it as if you had no help at all. God is still patient and encouraging even when you forget God.

Every time you sit down and emotionally waver on the path, the people that look up to you and are counting on you waver too. When you fall asleep for a moment, they fall asleep for a moment. You are not helping if you cannot stay awake spiritually and be consistent. What you do matters and how you think and feel matters. Everyone around you that cares about you, slides up and down on the roller coaster of your inconsistency, following you. They were initially inspired by your efforts and your clarity, but now they have to suffer the ride you take them on. Do you care about them? Then do not allow yourself mental vacations and emotional fits, because everyone will go on that ride with you almost at the exact same time. You are responsible for inspiring people and when they follow you that is an act of love and admiration. Do not disappoint people by failing them. Be helpful to people. God does not go on vacations and get irritable and take time off supporting all of life. God does not remove God's attention from the creation for an instant, or the creation would fall. Then down would come baby, cradle and all.

Jesus and Mary are becoming more divine each day and they are taking on more and more responsibility for souls each hour. They are growing and have been growing for 2000 years. What they must be like now is unimaginable to most mortal minds as they have encompassed the earth and become more powerful and loving. We have to run to catch up with them and we cannot afford to sit around and play promiscuously with things any more. We have to be accountable to them and what they want us to do. If we want to help them, then we have to have their consciousness and their vision. Then they can entrust us with small jobs until we develop to do more. Our love for Jesus and Mary makes us want to help and want to be prepared for more service to them.

There is no place in creation for a rest from consciousness. Your body may tire, but your consciousness and soul does not tire. We are in a continuous process of growth if we are not stubbornly trying to stop our own growth. If you let a little love in, then you will feel the impulse to expand and grow. Let a little more love in and you will feel a healing to your whole life taking place. Let a little more love in and you will overflow with good feelings and will be inspired to share that with others. Gradually you learn that it is more blessed to give what you are receiving than sitting and waiting to receive. As you give love, more love flows into you and you become aware of how blessed you and everyone is by God. You practice what you are learning and it never stops.

IT IS HARD TO BE A TEACHER

It is hard to be a teacher. God has given the teacher the experience of God that changes them permanently. In this experience, the love pours in and changes the very cells of one's body, the thought in one's mind and their perceptions open to perceive things that most people do not want to see. As the teacher opens, more of the plan and beauty of creation is available to them. This changes the expression and thoughts of the teacher so that their perspective is radically different than what most people understand about life. If I were an eagle flying 6 or 7 kilometers above the earth, I could see with my eagle eyes vast regions of the landscape that others who were walking around on the surface could not see. Those who have been blessed with an experience of light, love and consciousness are much like the eagle. They can spot movement at 75 kilometers and can look directly into the Sun without retinal damage. This same sight when looking at the feelings, thoughts and motives of people is just as keen. The teacher registers many different kinds of energies in people and becomes proficient at noticing things that most people do not see or feel. Is this a blessing or a curse, you might ask?

If the teacher sees things in people that do not want to know anything, then the teacher has to keep these things to himself. If people are interested in what the teacher perceives, then the teacher still has to weigh if the person can really receive what they see and feel because sometimes people want to know things and when they are told, they do not want to know those things. Their pride thinks they want to know everything and anything, but when they are told what the teacher sees, they are offended and angry about it. This is a dilemma. How much to tell people even if they claim to want to know. I am very cautious about telling people things because I have experienced many people claiming to want to know, but when they hear what the teacher says, they get offended, hurt or angry. So they did not want to know very much. Maybe they wanted to know just a little.

I am a firm believer in people volunteering for what they want to learn. I cannot force anyone and so I do not try to make anyone believe anything or do anything. God does not force anyone in creation and neither do I. I suggest and I try to influence; I wait for the right moment to say something. I cannot make anyone do anything or feel anything. What I can do is wait until you ask me to teach you. I can wait for you to invite me into an area of your life that you want help with. In the case of the priests, I assume you want me in all the areas of your lives and so I just teach whatever I see. I am here for the purpose of helping and raising you up into a consciousness that is possible for you. I know what to do, but you are in control of the process and the timing. When you are less frightened, then you will ask me for help.

Sometimes in a class I will slip a teaching in that might jostle a whole armory of concepts and in the next few days concepts will come tumbling down. I pray for that. Sometimes I tell someone else a story and relate the solution to their problem and many others in the class can identify with the story and take in the lesson. It is easier to learn sometimes if the lesson is indirect so that you do not feel pinned into a corner of having to own that it is your problem and the lesson is for you. I do not want people to feel that they have to change anything. You can change things if you want to. You will feel better if you change and you will be grateful for having some difficult weight lifted from your being and consciousness. The gratitude that you feel for being released from a sin or from a stuck pattern of thinking is in proportion to the depth of the change. The more you let go of, the more grateful you are. Jesus said, "Those who are forgiven of much, much will be required of them." The more you let love in, the more humble and grateful you will be and the more you will want to give back in love for God. Jesus used Mary Magdalene as an example of complete corruption in sin and vice. Once she accepted the healing and forgiveness for her condition, she became the most fiercely loyal and loving of disciples of Jesus. The more love you let in, the more connected your heart is to God.

The teacher has it hard because I know things that the Spirit of God shows me and I want to help. But then I have to wait, sometimes a long time, to be able to help you. I have to wait for you to be ready. That might take well-nigh forever. Many times I could relieve you of your burden and I suggest that you give it to us. I make the mistake of leaning towards you and putting my hand on the burden and trying to pull it just a little out of your hands or off your back. You snap at me angrily that I am taking your precious problem away. I get corrected for my presumption many times a day and I have to remember that people want their problems. It is sad, but it is your right to keep your problems. Almost without fail, the teacher says the fastest way through a difficult passage, the simplest solution to a problem and the clearest path through the jungle of your fears and doubts. Yet most of the time, people do not want the simplest, clearest fastest way through. We forget sometimes that people are happy to make people pay for their crimes, for the hurts and bruises of the past. They are not about to forgive and let things go without a fight. The teacher ends up being the one you fight with instead of your own tendency to hold a grudge and continue your resentment. Then the teacher receives your animosity and hostility even to the point of you lashing out verbally at them for wanting to be close to you.

I am hoping that I discourage you about wanting to be a teacher because it is very hard to take rejections. Rejections are constant, but Jesus and Mother Mary were the most rejected of any teacher who has ever lived. They were unappreciated, scoffed at and insulted constantly. The teacher can only hope that they get the same treatment even though it can hurt sometimes. But our job is helping and healing, not feeling sorry for ourselves. We know what to do if you come humbly for help. We know the process of letting go. We have given all to God, so we know what it is going to take for you to be liberated from your former life as a prisoner of your problems. We offer this to anyone. But you cannot follow us unless you let go of your problems and give them to God. You cannot carry all the baggage of your life into the Kingdom of God. You have to unpack all of those problems and let them go. Unpacking is humiliating because you spent so much time packing up all those things to carry them and you are kind of proud of being able to handle them. You get attached to the things you have been carrying around and you might feel undressed without them. We say, "Give them to Jesus." You respond, "I'm fine." We say, "No, you are weighed down with hurts and fears and anger." You say, "I'll manage." We say, "It will get harder to carry those things." You say, "Whatever." We shrug our shoulders and sigh because the conversation has ended. We pray.

There is a great danger on the path of taking credit for your development as if you did everything yourself. You are fooling yourself if you think that you can attain anything through your own personal efforts. Where is God if you think you did everything yourself? How can God bless your efforts if you do not invite God in to help and guide you? You see, the whole business of doing your own thing and having things go your way was the way we got into trouble in the first place. Adam and Eve wanted to do things on their own and in their own way. We have toiled, labored and suffered ever since and now we have a way back to being helped by God if we would only bend our knees and humbly accept the help. God cannot do anything for us unless we open our hearts and ask for help. Jesus and Mary encourage us to ask and they are so willing to be there to help us when we open to their graces.

CHANGES, CHANGES, CHANGES

We are entering into a time of tremendous change and we are going to need to be grounded in something real in order to manage them. The first of these changes is personal. The second is spiritual. The third change is global. Any way you look at this, you will have to become graceful and welcoming of change. If you were born at this time in the history of the planet, you came in with a pretty good idea of the vast number of changes you would have to experience while being here. Your soul knew that or you would not have come at this time. So, any of you who think that you were not informed about all the changes, remember that your soul already saw them ahead of your conscious mind and body. That could be relaxing.

The first change is personal. The way you live in your body and feel what you feel is shifting month to month. In the last 40 years, the recommendations of what people eat have changed at least three times. It used to be lots of meat and potatoes with high levels of sugars and dairy. Then many people ate non-fat, then many became vegetarians, which included a spiritual inclination to be more sensitive, and then there was the non-carbohydrate phase, and many others. Everyone is trying to get the formula for physical health right to live a long time. I am not sure why they want to do that since most people are unhappy and miserable. Anyway, there is the dietary change, the gluten free, non-dairy etc. that continue to be innovative. Then we have the annual change in our cellphone with the new models coming out and new ways to be tracked and monitored via GPS location and the learning curve on the new technology. There is no tradition in technology as it up levels itself and gets more and more sophisticated each year which requires users to update and re-learn all the time. The education of new devices is part of our culture now and required if you are going to keep up and have the latest services, skills and slick aps that are recommended (sold) to you. It is a fact of our life now with almost 6 billion people with cell phones on earth that we are not going to be able to go back to the old ways of telephone lines or being able to remember the ten digits of our phone numbers again. Devices remember everything for you. We have been sold on everything needing to be at our fingertips, everything seamless and easy. This is great technology and it has a tendency to lull us to sleep. We do not need to leave our office chair to walk to the store or go out in the natural air to shop for food or greet people at the market. We don't have to walk because people deliver things to our door.

In many ways, we have changed the natural pattern of our lives many times in the last 40 years and our physical bodies have to adjust to this or be left behind. In the last hundred years, we have gone from an agricultural society to industrial and now to a communications society. Our physical bodies do not need to lift, drag, pull and stress out any longer. We use our bodies much differently now. There is a tendency to just float along and look good and try to eat things that don't put on weight without all that inconvenient exercise regimen. But we need to exercise or the tension builds up and we get out of balance. The body likes movement and work, so we have to find ways to make that happen in order to stay in good health.

Spiritual change involves an inner shift in consciousness and awareness that blows open the doors to your perception and awakens you to meaning and movements of energy that you could not know before. Seeing the world from the point of view of the victim where things happen to you is much different from viewing the world as a canvas where you paint your story and move energy in creation. Being passive is for an animal-like consciousness, whereas being fully human is to become a co-creator and making things happen using God's energy to create with. If you are

156

on a spiritual path of some kind, especially one like ours, you are being asked to change the way you move around in your body, the way you think and the way you move your consciousness. You are asked to notice things about life, people and yourself that you were never asked to see before. This awareness changes the cells in your body and brain to feel things you did not register before and to observe things that used to be out of your awareness. This changes your body and brain simply by the practice of new ideas, thoughts and feelings. Then we ask you to change how you react to others which changes the habits you were taught. You are disrupting the habitual way you are used to being, seeing and acting in the world. If you hate change, then you will hate planet earth and hate a spiritual path. The lack of connection to God was caused by a separation of consciousness that can only be remedied by re-connecting. You can look at any change as being a disruption or you can accept change as a welcome raise in consciousness. You might be striving to be different in how you open to other people to receive them and give to them. We ask you to stop seeing them through the lens of your fears and anger so that you can really appreciate them for who they are and not who you want them to be. The change comes about through love and appreciation.

In the 1960's and 1970's people thought they were really evolving if they were no longer prejudiced about someone's skin color. Then they noticed they still held on to tremendous resentment for differing opinions about religion or politics, and all their anger came flying up in their awareness. This showed that they were not as evolved as they thought they were in reality. Now we have to realize that the whole human race is really a sister and a brother to us and there is no sensible reason for any differences, no justification for any entitlement that one is a better human being than anyone else. This is a step up even for people on a spiritual path as they pride fully feel at times that they are better than other people. The reasonable thing to feel is that you would like your peace to be experienced by everyone and you pray that the love you feel inside would be everyone's experience. That is a great blessing to others to hold that consciousness so that it will come to be.

There are many spiritual changes that occur with a student on a spiritual path. They are asked to shelve and hold in abeyance their own opinions about what is real and what is lasting until they have the experience of God within them. They are asked to trust someone who has had that experience until they have their own awakening experience. During the trusting time, they must admit that they don't really know many things absolutely and have to let someone lead them to that experience. It takes quite a bit of time to deepen in trust and no matter how much trust you think you have, you hold out deep, dark areas that no one is allowed to enter because you are terrified in that place. That is why it takes time. That frozen tundra of terror takes tremendous heat and love to melt and lay bare the wound. Some don't get to that stage because they are too traumatized to allow anyone into that place to love them there. The risk is so great that the very person they hope in and the one who they feel they could open to might hurt them and that is the crux of the problem. They have to die to their old life of protection and mistrust and open to love. We all had to do that in our own process with our teacher and there is no way through it without that dying to oneself. You can see how that would be a revolutionary change in your being to do that.

Other spiritual changes involve the way you look at life and the world. When you are young and narcissistic, everything is about you and how you feel about things. Then you notice other people have feelings and then you begin to see that everyone has a similar struggle to find who they are and how to be happy. It is a big world. It is like when you were the top of your high school class and you went to college and all those tops of the class were your class mates now and they are so bright, intelligent and motivated. You become depressed because you are just like them and not so special. You are just normal in that batch of bright lights. That is the humbling that people on the spiritual path receive. They are not so spiritual compared to others more advanced. They are definitely not so spiritual as Jesus and Mother Mary and that is humbling and shows this infinite path of developing consciousness that everyone is on. It is all relative to where you are and what lessons you are learning. In relation to the galactic beings, those suns that have joined and unified in one mind and purpose at the center of vast billions of suns, leading them in their development, our little sun, outlying on the edge of this Milky Way galaxy is kind like a child that just started elementary school, learning to love. The levels of spiritual consciousness go on infinitely in the grander scheme of God's life. What seems so big to us and so revelatory is a blip of awakening that is beautiful, but on the grand scale, it is not much. But we celebrate all changes in consciousness because they are the step you are on and it is wonderful. Your spiritual changes bring you great compassion because the ones who want to know so much seem foolish to those who are having great love experiences and openings of the heart. We compassionately smile inside when we see so much stretching to know information and tidbits of truths that pack your skull with knowledge. We are looking to when your heart ignites and explodes in the birth of a new sun in your spiritual sky. That is a glorious moment when your heart opens and you no longer find such fascination in knowing things and spouting tidbits of truths so fashionable in worldly eyes.

You change from a competitor to a spiritual athlete of love. You move from a jealous comparer of yourself to other people, to one who celebrates and appreciates all movement of growth no matter in what place on the planet. You celebrate and support all the movements of life. All the ambitions and desperate attempts to be good, better and best move aside to settle in to accepting the gifts God gives you as well as the work God gives you to do, without pining for what someone else has. You give over to God and let go to God's will for you.

The world changes are the third change which is upon us now. We are whirling into two great powers clashing against each other. On the one hand, the spiritually awakening human beings are seeing the end of all the world powers that steal from their people and wage violent wars to get what they want. Those days will be over soon. Peace will reign on the earth after the last eruption of darkness and meanness explodes. The bloated lords of power that have ripped people off for a hundred years are going to be destroyed by their own hand. There is no reason for war on this planet anymore. We are bankrupt as a country because we have used all our resources to promote our ego as the world police. Actually, we are the uneducated bully of the world, the aggressor that pompously thinks it is justified in interfering in the lives of other peoples. The changes are coming fast, faster than you think. They are at our door. The United States passed into law that any citizen can be arrested, detained, tortured and killed for no reason and without the due process of law, meaning no trial by a jury of their peers. The First and Fourth Amendment rights are no more. All the cellphones and emails transmissions are recorded to make sure no one is speaking out against the powers that be. The law to arrest anyone who says anything against the lords of power over the internet has been placed before Congress. This would mean that any suspicious statement might cause your assets to be frozen, your services cut off and you to be arrested without due process. The monitoring of the internet is the threat we exist in now. If that happens, the people will have been enslaved completely.

Many people know this is the real threat, the loss of freedom of speech and ideas. Are you willing to educate yourself on these things and not put your head in the sand? The economies of the world were built on the backs of slaves serving the needs of these lords of money. All the wars were actually greed in the name of power. The spiritual people are sick of this and will not cooperate with this any longer. We pray for peace. We prayed for the corruption to be revealed and the next day news articles came out demonstrating the very things we have been talking about. It happens every time we pray for the corruption to be shown up in the world press. Our world is corrupt along with the powers that make it so. Most of the congress and senate of the United States need to be removed and replaced by honest people. We need to start over with a new President, new government and a new transition to peace. All military engagements in other countries should stop and those soldiers come home, even the contractors that they do not call soldiers should come home as well. The lords of money have used our politicians and bought them with bribes to give them our military to be used to disrupt countries the lords of money want to exploit and steal from.

Whether the people of the United States completely change is not so important because we will not be able to continue to print fake money to support these ridiculous wars. Our money is fake and we have been broke for a long time. We now have ¼ of our people below the poverty line. When are we going to wake up? The change is upon us and we have been knocked out and we are the last to know that we are on our knees, almost unconscious. We think we are fighting the good fight, but our arms won't move anymore. This is why we are preparing ourselves to be more self-sufficient, industrious, hard-working and innovative. We need to be ready for the demise of our country and the services that we took for granted while we were bullying the whole world. The whole financial fabric of the world is dissolving and we have to get how significant that is. Wealth needs to be based on something of value, not on imaginary paper like the Federal Reserve created. The lords of money want a world war so that they can manage two-thirds less people. They want the deaths of two-thirds of the people because it will be easier to manage 2 billion than 7 billion. They keep trumping up the need for war and now the focus is Syria, Russia and China. They are not our enemies, the few lords of money are. Pray these lords of money are revealed for all the horrors they have inflicted on the human race, on every country of the world and that they be found out and their lies exposed. Pray they are arrested and convicted of their crimes against humanity. Pray that all those who aided them through their greed and ignorance be discovered, exposed and arrested as well. Their ways must end.

When this happens, and it will, we will have a new world, with a whole new set of challenges. You will have to get along with everyone or you will be left behind. You will have to change and care about other people and really learn to be at peace with each other. Love will reign on the earth after a great convulsion of desperate struggle with the servants of the lords of power. It is happening now, so get a real relationship with God so you can be at peace and in love. Everything we do is designed to help you be a strong son or daughter of God, with love in your heart and compassion in your mind. Peace should guide all of your movements as you learn to be a non-reactive agent of change on the planet.

HOW WE ARE DIFFERENT

The order that trained me began in 1968, and was called the Holy Order of Mans. It no longer exists because the members of that order did not have the discipline, stamina and spiritual formation to withstand more than twelve years. Many did not serve more than a few years at most. Most of the members of that order were in their early twenties when Father Paul connected with them and they came in inexperienced, uneducated and without any real training in a profession. When they started families they did not have careers yet and were living poorly without any health insurance. The service they did perform was impressive given that they had limited work experience. Being so young, it is not surprising that many of them could not persist in their service for very long. I am grateful that Father Paul started the Holy Order of Mans and I learned many things from them that I continue to appreciate and live by to this day.

Some have claimed that we have patterned ourselves on that order, but we actually have very little resemblance to them now since we have been moved by Jesus and Mary into what they want us to be. There are similarities in the sacraments, the vows and the student-teacher relationship, but from that point on, we are quite different. Two main points stand out for me as major differences. One is that we do the psychological part of helping people to heal deep wounds from childhood and from misconceptions of safety and protection of the ego. Most people spent years with caregivers experiencing treatment that was scary or painful. Parents handled things badly. We reacted and acted out in anger, we recoiled in shame, we shut down and became passive and then proceeded to treat ourselves terribly. We were either scared, angry, feeling alone and abandoned or just plain terrified growing up. Our pride and ego developed strong protections from the pain of this mistreatment and we lost touch with ourselves over the years. After we grew old enough to make different decisions, we became stubborn and decided the treatment we received was wrong. This bolstered up our pride and made us self-righteousness and twisted. Our ego became vigilant about anything difficult and we reacted to anyone who made us suffer or work to achieve things.

As a grown up, we are still reacting in pride to anything hard and challenging, anyone who is mean or insensitive. We lash out at them in our pride and decide to not cooperate when things seem unfair. The main reaction is being touchy and avoiding anything hard. Each of you has developed a vigilant ego where you are ready to react if you are inconvenienced in the least. In the life of a student, those areas of your touchiness get a great deal of attention so you can be less of an ego reacting and more of a real loving human being. You learn how to be a disciple who knows how to give and serve and care for other people. There is a great deal of hurt you have to forgive and a massive amount of ego you have to let go of in order to be a real disciple of Jesus and Mary. The old order did not know how to do this work, so people would be moved up spiritually and still have these unworked and unhealed areas that continued to act out in relationships with other people. We are dedicated to not let you be in a position of influence and authority if you still have these unhealed parts inside of you.

The other point that characterizes the difference in what we do with the old way is that we emphasize real feelings in our relationships with each other. We value honesty, integrity and love more than position and self-defense. Being real means you are not an ego strutting around like a peacock in bloom. Being real means you have relaxed your need to be vigilant around abuse and people being mean to you. Being real means you are willing and able to share the vulnerable parts of yourself without fearing other people's response or having the mistaken idea that you have to protect yourself from others. Being real means you can love others without worrying that they won't treat you right. In the old order, the brothers and sisters did not share themselves or reveal very much about themselves to each other. They kept to themselves and were in a silent competition with each other about who was going to attain the spiritual initiations before someone else. I did not see this at the time but became aware of it as I realized the members of that order had little practice interacting in a loving and open way with other people. We have changed all that.

Our definition of intelligence is the ability to get along with other people. If you are kind of a loner, you are still in some subtle way protecting yourself. Shyness is different from being a loner. Shyness is a beginning caution that is not sure others want to know you. That is fine, but you have to move out of shyness into sharing yourself unabashedly with others. In our order, everyone is safe or they cannot stay here long. Sometimes a student will get angry at someone but the priests have the necessary skills to help resolve any differences and help you work these problems out. Differences happen between people, but if your pride and ego are not involved in the interaction, things work out very smoothly. In the old order there was tremendous unspoken competition for attainment. We do not want that as it is pride disguised as devotion, just as in the Franciscan order there was competition among some of the brothers for who could fast longer or torture themselves more severely than their brother. That is not okay and we discourage that behavior when we see it. No pride or fear can make any of your decisions or guide any of your actions or words. That is darkness and we are watchdogs to make sure that those negative strands of ego that pride and fear promote are rejected from our behavior and from our spiritual community. When you first become part of our order and begin learning, you are full of many concepts, feelings and ways of being that will ultimately have to change. You have to become like Jesus and Mary and that will mean a complete change from insecurity to peace. You will have to replace meanness with patience and love. You will be asked to learn acceptance of others instead of hostility, criticism and judgment. You will learn to forgive because it re-connects you with God's love. God cannot forgive you if you will not forgive others. In most new students, there are many people that you hold resentment for and all of them have to be forgiven. But you cannot just give a superficial forgiveness; it has to be deep and real.

The more you are aware of how ego works, how pride and fear works, the less likely you will be to be tempted when the trials magnify on the earth. We are in a very serious transition point on the planet and those who will be following fear and pride, in other words, darkness, will be taking sides against those who follow love, realness, truth and integrity. It will not be advertised, it will just happen. It is happening now and very quickly at that. When a country spends more on the military than it does on the quality of life of its citizens; then that country has decided to enslave its people for the benefit of the ones that rule. Rome did the very same thing so that they could conquer most of the earth. Sell the people on being the most powerful country and then enlist all wealth and resources for the preservation of that military prowess and the people suffer. Sell the people on dangers in the world and then stroke their pride that we have the most sophisticated weapons to protect us from those dangers. We create the dangers and we are the most dangerous in the world. The U.S. is the most dangerous of all the countries in the world and the most disrespectful of the rights of their citizens and the needs of the people.

Our order is unique in many ways. The teacher and priests of our order do not engage in sexual relationships with students. There is no sexual acting out among the priests or students or they will not be able to continue being in a position of influence. We do not have power struggles among the leaders as that would be a very bad example to others of how Jesus and Mary are Co-Redeemers.

Forty years ago, a spiritual order came into manifestation that was revolutionary and brought a closeness to Jesus and an honoring of Mother Mary that had not been in the consciousness of humanity since Jesus and Mary were here. It was the beginning of an awakening that did not come into fruition even though it was a start of something new. We have taken up that call and have allowed Jesus and Mary to evolve the expression of the mystical life into what we have today. We have been persecuted for our intensity, our purity and our faithfulness to the revelation given to us by Jesus and Mary. We will not compromise our mission or change our direction based on the opinions of people in the world. We need to stay focused on the preparation of people to be part of the change that is coming on our planet. We need great faith and trust in God. We need much less ego and competitive energy. We need more love and acceptance of the good within each sister and brother on the earth. Our job is to be the light of the world and to be the compassionate healer energy that we feel from Jesus and Mary. We are their hands and feet as we are in a position to truly bring their blessings to everyone.

THE BLOOD OF CHRIST

Each one of us has committed enumerable sins for which we need forgiveness. Sin is the action of separating from God who made us. God decided what sin is; we did not get to decide that. God decided what was good and evil before we existed and our opinions about it do not change the nature of good or evil. If we separate from God's love and obedience to God, we sin. Free will allows us to choose to align ourselves with God or to do things our own way. God longs for us to come back home and be in union with God. In our deepest heart, we long for this separation to end and we want to come back home at some point. Because of our sins, we need forgiveness in order to come back into union with God. I will talk later on about the fact that we need deliverance from the power of sin.

Our conscience should burn when we separate from God and if we are sensitive and not completely shut down spiritually, it does burn when we sin. We need forgiveness for what we have done in thought or action. God sent Jesus and Mary to secure our forgiveness as a substitute for Adam and Eve's sin by paying it off through their obedience. Jesus' blood paid it since sin is our inheritance from Adam and Eve, our first parents. Jesus stood in as our substitute, dying on the cross, to pay our debt to God and start us on the road back to oneness with God. But our sins caused a barrier to relationship with God causing an estrangement making us unrecognizable to God. Jesus had to pay for that sense of guilt with his love and his blood. There is pure life in Jesus' blood that had to be poured out for us in order to atone for everyone's sins. His death totally satisfied God and this became so precious to God that God considered the sin of Adam paid. The sacrifice of Jesus and

169

Mary was acceptable to God as payment for our sins and evidence of the atonement and redemption of everyone.

As soon as we see our error and feel our guilty conscience, our faith weakens and we have trouble facing God. We need cleansing and atonement to resolve the block we placed between ourselves and God. A clear conscience is obtained by the fact of Jesus shedding his blood through obedience to God. God looks at the offering of Jesus and Mary and is completely satisfied with it. God's acceptance is the basis upon which we may approach and have no more consciousness of sins. Doing penance or feeling bad about yourself will not make you holier. The mistaken idea that you can do anything of yourself to make yourself better is Satan's strategy to confuse you about your merits and make you fail. The temptation is to work on you to improve yourself. You will fail if you do things on your own. God will withdraw from you if you think you can do things by yourself.

Adam and Eve's disobedience threw us out of the garden and we became estranged to God. The blood of Jesus cleanses us of every sin. When we hope to have some goodness of our own, then we buy into the accusation of Satan that we expect our good conduct to make us safe. The Blood alone makes us right with God. When we know this, we are completely held in God's love and re-united with God again.

We need the Blood for forgiveness and we need the Cross for deliverance. We will talk of deliverance later. "To set your mind on the flesh is death, but to set your mind on the Spirit is life and peace." Romans 8:6 Jesus bore our sins on the Cross and obtained forgiveness, justification and reconciliation. Through one person we have all become sinners because we were born inheriting Adam and Eve's tendency to sin. Through the obedience of one, we all become righteous. When we first come to the spiritual life, we are concerned about what we have done in our lives. We are also distressed about what we find when we look within ourselves. We try to please God but find something fighting us inside that wants to do something unloving. We have little humility and act most selfishly. Through the Fall of Adam and Eve we were all separated and made wrong and unable to please God. We became sinners. We derive our existence from our first parents who were sinful. By their disobedience we all entered into death and despair. Our hope is in Christ.

Bondage to sin came from being born offspring of Adam and Eve, who became other than what God intended them to be. We were unable to please God because we are all involved in Adam and Eve's sin. We lost everything because of our separation. We were thrown out of the garden and were not permitted to partake of the Tree of Life. Through the death and sacrifice of one we have been delivered from death and separation from God. We have died to sin. *"Do you not know that all of us who were baptized into Christ Jesus were baptized in Christ's death?"* (Romans 6:3)

Now we are in Christ because one died for all. When Jesus was crucified, we were crucified and when he died as our representative, we died as well. Jesus included us in his death. God included all of us in Christ's death. We were also included in Jesus Christ's resurrection. Jesus and Mary gathered up all that was in Adam and Eve and took it to the judgment and to death. Our history ends with the Cross and our life begins with the resurrection. Jesus died as our substitute and so we have all died. Our sins were canceled by his Blood because it was an accomplished fact. *"We died with Christ."* Romans 6:8 Jesus took me to the cross so that when he died, I died with him. God decided this sacrifice was sufficient for you as well and it does not depend on your feelings or your opinion. You have died and the old you is done.

Our transformation can never occur by force of will or effort. It can only be accomplished by accepting the fact that Jesus Christ died on the cross. We may try to suppress sin by overcoming it; but God's way is to remove the sinner. We cannot make ourselves stronger and tougher, but we must be made weaker and weaker. God sets us free from sin's dominion not by strengthening our ego but by crucifying us. God does not help us do things better, but sets us aside by opening the eyes of our hearts to see what we have in Christ.

"We know that our old life died with Christ on the cross so that our sinful selves would have no power over us and we would not be slaves to sin." (Romans 6:6) This is final - things have been canceled and done. We are dead and must take account that we have died to our old life. When Jesus was on the Cross, we were there with him. Faith is the assurance that we have a substantiated reason to hope. If we were included in Christ's death, then we were included in the forgiveness of our sins. Jesus secured our deliverance. Our sins are dealt with by his Blood and we ourselves are dealt with by the Cross.

Through the death and resurrection of Jesus Christ, the body that sins has become unemployed even though sin is still around. The person who served sin has been put to death and no longer is an instrument for it. Redemption means that we are redeemed and refashioned as clean and whole before God. God can recognize us now the way God made us and we are not estranged anymore. We are cleansed and made whole, but what do we do now. We still have tendencies, habits and patterns within us that are practiced and indulgent. Our former life has been forgiven because Jesus procured it for us. So there is more because we need deliverance from the power and tendency to sin which we received from our ancestors. Forgiveness of our sins and regeneration of our being is not based on our merits, but simply and completely on the merits of Jesus

Christ. We have not done anything at all to receive justification and blessings in the eyes of God. We must accept that fact that Jesus and Mary did everything and put our faith in them.

Jesus' death freed us from the law. As soon as we try to please God on our own (meaning in the flesh or in the ego), we place ourselves under the law once again. As long as we are trying to do anything at all, God cannot act through us. God waits for us to be at the end of our strength in doing things by ourselves. *"The flesh profits nothing."* If you think that if you meditate, read or pray more then you will be a better person, you are still depending on yourself and you will fail. We are to be totally dependent on God in order to thrive. God is the only doer or actor in creation. When we let the Holy Spirit move, it means we trust the Holy Spirit to do in me what we cannot do by ourselves. Our personal effort and strain is not necessary and will not carry us into real victory. Grace will.

Satan desires to tempt you to act on your own behalf, to make you think you can do things by yourself. Sin, self-reliance and individualism were the means to kill God's purpose in human beings. Your victory involves not doing anything of our own will. If you have to exert a great deal of effort in your life, it means you have not really chosen the way you want to be yet. If you use willpower to please God, you have not learned to trust God yet and cannot experience the new life that would like to be in you. If you yield to the dictates of the flesh and ego, you will be brought into immediate conflict with God. *"The true children of God are those who let God's Spirit lead them."* Romans 8:14 God separates you out of the world to be holy and you cease your old life. You stop having confidence in your own body and ego.

The process is this: our sins are forgiven; we are dead with Christ; we are helpless by nature; and we rely completely on the indwelling Spirit. Then we are one in the body of Christ.

"..the Lamb of God is about to be sacrificed and His Blood is about to mark the doorposts of hearts, and the angel of the Lord will pass without striking those who have upon themselves, and with love, the Blood of the sacrificed Lamb, that is about to be raised on the cross bar, like the precious metal snake, to be the sign for those wounded by the infernal snake, to be salvation for those who look at it with love."
Vol. 9, p. 227

THE CROSS OF CHRIST

1943 Notebooks, p. 424

"When the Son of God, the one who loves you, comes into the midst of the multitudes marked with his indelible sign, that sign which is more glorious than a royal crown because it gives you a heavenly royalty as sons and daughters and heirs of the Most High, he finds that few have fought against instinct and Satan or washed away the stains of Satan and instinct by repentance so as to have that sign of predestination clean and active. To those few, the beloved of my heart, I, the Son of God, to whom all power of judgment is handed over by the Father, come to impart a baptism of burning fire, which blazes and consumes all humanity in them to make their spirits free and render them capable of receiving the Spirit, who speaks.

".... The tendrils are the weak, the lukewarm, who want to benefit from the communion of the saints, but without striving to contribute even a minimal effort to it. They are the spiritually slothful, those who always need stimuli, support, and warmth to lead their poor spiritual lives; without the factors of different aids, they would crawl on the ground, unable to tend towards heaven and would be trampled on by the Evil One, trampled, I say, not caught. They are scorned even by him. He doesn't care about them because he knows that by themselves they slay their souls."

We need deliverance from the power of sin, that principle that works in us and shows what we are. In the Blood of Jesus we receive the forgiveness of our sins. It deals with what we have done. The Cross deals with what we are and strikes at the root of our capacity for sin. In the New Testament, Blood is connected to atonement over a hundred times. God was satisfied with Jesus and Mary's sacrifice. The Blood can wash away our sins and forgive them, but cannot wash away the old person. The Cross is necessary to crucify us to deal with the sinner. We are sinners by inheritance, but after forgiveness, we still have to be delivered from what we are. What we have done is wrong because we came from Adam and Eve, and now we see that we are not right with God.

The real temptation of Satan trapped human beings into taking a course of action where we could develop our own personality and not rely on God. Anything we are able to do without reliance on God springs from the life of the body and the ego and resists dependence on God. Everything we do apart from God is counted as nothing. Jesus said, "I, of myself, can do nothing." What is born of the flesh is flesh, so all the situations we find ourselves that seem like we are enough on our own, we can count as nothing. When we have areas in our being that are closed to God, places in our heart that are too delicate for God and areas of our thoughts where our pride cannot allow interference, then we are defeated already. God is not allowed to influence us there. We are actually wrong for having this attitude because we are not open to God helping us there. Adam and Eve wanted to develop themselves without God's help. Satan always tries to get us to act by ourselves, on our own. Jesus turned all that around by submitting each temptation to a total denial of letting his personality govern his actions. He was obedient only to God. Most people have a secret love or some human ambition that gets in the way of obediently following the will of God with trust. Jesus said, *"Whoever wants to follow me, let them deny themselves and take up their cross and follow me. For whoever will save their life will lose it; but whoever will lose their life for my sake and the Gospel's, will save it. For what shall it profit you if you gain the whole world and lose your soul?"* Mark 8-34-35

We have been for forgiven for what we have done. Our bondage came by birth and our deliverance through death

176

on our own personal Cross will bring emancipation and death of our old self.

Remember Paul's words, *"Do you not know that all of us who have been baptized in Christ Jesus were baptized in Christ's death."* (Romans 6:3)

"So if anyone is in Christ, they are a new creation: everything old has passed away; behold all things become new." (2 Corinthians 5:17)

We must die with Christ and praise him for bearing us on the Cross with him. The part of us that we detest is crucified in our acceptance and removed from our lives. We have died with Christ on the Cross and are dead. God used the Cross as the means to put an end to the old things and to bury our old self.
"When we were baptized, we were buried with Christ and shared his death. So, just as Christ was raised from the dead by the wonderful power of the Father-Mother God, we also can live a new life." Romans 6:4-5

When should you ask for baptism? When you see that God's way is perfect and that you deserve to die, and when you truly believe that God has already crucified you. Once you are really convinced that you are quite dead, and then apply for baptism. You are ready to be counted as among the dead and you accept the sentence of death given to you by God for your inherited life in Adam and Eve. The union with Christ is yours through the death and resurrection of Jesus Christ. Jesus' death becomes yours and the death of everything that is not God becomes yours as well. You are united to Christ and given a new life. Your life now belongs to God if you will accept it. You present your whole being to God and you are not your own anymore.

The word 'holy' means set apart. We become holy when we are anointed and consecrated, not by any effort on our part or any suppression of badness. Giving our whole anatomy over to God is holiness. That is the day we do not belong to ourselves anymore because we have been grafted in or adopted by Jesus and Mary. If we are careful how much we are giving or praying and calculating how loving we are, then we cut ourselves off from God. God owns us now since God paid for us with the Blood and the Cross of God's own son. We are God's creation and God's property and can no longer act out willfully. God wants your very life. That means God wants our cherished ideas and opinions, our valued relationships and our precious identification with our work. God takes this very seriously, so should we. We are to find no fault with how God wants to use us. Remember when the disciples brought bread to Jesus, he broke it and offered it to those who were hungry. When we offer ourselves to Jesus, he will break what is offered. This happens when things start to go wrong and we protest at how much is asked of us. We sometimes criticize our ministers and even God. At this point we are no good for God because we have not decided permanently to let ourselves die to our old life and we are not much use for the world because we are still broken. Do not find fault with God's use of us. We should accept whatever God dishes out to us and praise God for trying to make any use of us at all. God's purpose in the redemption is to give glory to God and to give glory to all the children God created.

Jesus Christ was the only begotten Son of God because he was the first. There were no other sons that had been justified and glorified up to that point. He was the first. God wishes for all God's children to be begotten sons and daughters of God so that God can glorify them. This is the new life God wants for all humanity after we separated and wants us dead to our old life. After Jesus ascended, the Holy Spirit came and endowed the disciples with power from on high. The Spirit was poured out on us because of God's goodness. When we changed our hearts and came back to God, our bodies were made a temple of God.

"Do you not know that you are God's temple and that God's Spirit lives in you?" (1 Corinthians 3:16)

LET US TEACH YOU

Some of you are just beginning the real spiritual path. I can imagine your ego not liking this thought very much because you have many experiences that you know brought you to this point. In a way, everyone is just beginning because the growth and expansion of consciousness that is coming is much more than what you have experienced before. Each day is a new possibility of experience and unfoldment. Each minute holds an opportunity for you to be more fully your soul accepting more of God to express through you. If you are new to our particular spiritual school, then you are just beginning. I am not discounting the experiences you have had this lifetime and all the growth that has moved you to this place. I am aware that many people were involved in getting you nudged closer and closer to this spiritual community and that if it were not for those varied experiences, you would not be here today. The past is the compost bed in which the plants of today are found. It would also be necessary to mention other lives and past experiences of your soul in other bodies in order to round out the picture of who you are and how you got here today. Most of you are not that conscious of your past lifetimes of experience even if some psychic mentioned a few things to you along the way. I don't personally hold much stock in what psychics have to say since they have very low reliability. The psychics are listening to very underdeveloped, earthbound spirits for the most part.

Since we are all beginning on this step that we are on and it is different from the step your sister or brother is on, let's accept a very basic teaching: God is the only actor and doer in all of creation. God in you is the main character in this human story. The beginning involves some humility. You have only the experience you have. You have only the knowledge and understanding that you have acquired. You have only the consciousness that you have developed so far. You can evaluate that consciousness a little by examining your certainty of God's presence within you. Do you absolutely know God within and have you seen God? Don't be vague about this answer or try to be tricky in stretching the truth. You have seen God or you haven't. It is very simple. Jesus said, "If your eye be single, your whole body will be full of light." Have you seen the Light? Do you know what it is beyond having heard about it? Have you had this experience of the Light filling your whole body and charging it up? If you have had the experience, then you know about the light. It is the same with knowing God. Jesus said, "Blessed are the pure in heart, for they shall see God." He did not say that you will feel God or have a good feeling for God, or that your belief in God will grow stronger. He said you will see God. He was clear and simple in his teachings and did not wax symbolic as many of the earthly ministers have surmised. He meant exactly that you would see God. Have you seen God? If you haven't, then you have some growing to do. If you haven't seen God, then you have impurities, desires and contaminations on your heart. You still want things you should not want. You still desire things that choke your soul and cloud your consciousness. That is impurity which will prevent you from seeing God.

Since some of you are new to our spiritual community, I want to help you know what to strive for and what to work for in your process of moving to becoming a real student. Some might find that being a student too difficult and demanding. We want to offer our teachings to everyone even if people did not want to immerse themselves in everything we do and practice. But some of you are definitely willing to become real students in a teacher-student relationship. If you are, then you see clearly that doing what you are told and letting a teacher in to your heart to love you and see you is critical to the process of spiritual development.

I want to say for those of you that have the eastern state of mind and have studied eastern spiritual traditions, that the concept of striving and attaining and acquiring is not the language they speak. They are not concerned with these things. At the same time, the eastern teachings tell you to meditate and be still and mindful in order to attain enlightenment. They tell you to stop things in order to attain them. The Christian mystical path teaches a much more active and positive way. You must have the mind of Christ and you must love. This action will take you far away from the mind of the world and place you at the feet of God. Most of the concepts that you have read and learned about from various eastern traditions and others will have to be placed on the metaphorical shelf for some time. This is for the simple reason that those ways of thinking and those concepts have not gotten you very far spiritually. They have merely replaced an old concept with anew one which seems fresher but is as empty as the other. If a concept does not move along to an experience, then it is a dead form and useless from God's point of view. A concept might be a bridge, it might be useful to strive for something, but if it does not turn into an experience, then it is meaningless.

If you enter into our school as a student, not merely as a visitor checking things out, then you are serious about your spiritual life. You want a direct experience. We are not a church. We are not even that religious when it comes down to it. We are too practical for that. We have learned that unless something happens, nothing happens. We have learned that unless you open and let go of the old, the new cannot take place. Unless you replace your worn out mind with a newborn spirit, you will not grow into what God envisioned for you when you were first built. God has rights over the creation. You are not autonomous and isolated. God is within you and God is all around you and you will never get away from that. You could wall yourself off in darkness and if you hate God enough, you will be separated permanently from the one that loves you and wants your growth. God wants you and loves you or God would not have created you. Most people in the world do not even feel God much less believe in God. People are free to believe anything they want and there is a lot of evidence that people are doing just that. We are an experiential path which means something happens to you that you could not have created by yourself and that it is bigger than you. God is bigger than you. Your soul is bigger and more important than your body or your feelings or your thoughts. Your soul generates your body, mind and feelings and so is higher than those things. The thoughts, feelings and body are expressions of your soul and so are less than soul.

If you wish to become a student in our school, then you will have to submit yourself to being led and taught. That is necessary. You cannot be given the deeper teachings about who you are unless you have humbled yourself to one who knows. The humility required is not subservience or blind faith. It is understanding that you must follow someone who knows if you are to be able to know yourself. This is the test of humility: can you do what you are told. Can you follow the spiritual exercises as they are given or must you think up your own clever and creative ways to not do what you are given? Must you emphasize your ego or can you just follow what you are directed to do? If you are scared and nervous, then you are not ready to be a student. If you are still angry at those in authority, then you are not ready to be a student yet. If you are scared or angry, then your pride is operating at full throttle and you want someone to pay for your earlier pain. That is a different energy than one who knows they don't know and needs someone to help them so that they can know. Knowledge only comes from experience. You cannot experience peace, bliss, love, joy or God if you are bracing and angry and prideful. It can't be done, because you are blocking the very thing you think you want.

If you feel completely loved, then let that soak in more and more until you are completely love yourself. I am not talking about smaltzy love or spacey love. I am talking about love that has muscles, love that has power in it, love that can take insult and rejection, love that does not falter because of some minor setback. The way you start letting love in is getting close to the teacher. Their consciousness is like a fire that will purify and a love that will penetrate into you and hold for you the image of God that you were created in. They do not accentuate your negative points. They look to the good in you. They see the God in you. They work on your souls to emphasize your real nature and not your outer stupidity. Your outer ego and ideas are almost completely worthless from God's point of view. Your ideas, your concepts, your opinions, your conclusions are almost always short-sighted and silly. You are much more than those concepts and ideas. You are much more powerful than some kind of idiosyncrasy. You are a divine being and you need to unfold that in order to understand who you are.

In your beginning stages of growth with us, you will learn many things and hear lots of new ways of expressing ancient truths. Those truths aren't yours until you experience them. Don't make the mistake of thinking that if you express them well, that you have really understood them or assimilated them. Many people talk and talk and nothing happens. Some people talk and things take place. Some speak the Word and healings happen. Some speak the Word and God moves inside of you. I would suggest that you speak what is helpful to others. Speak what is kind and necessary and what is true. But generally, if you do not know something, speak a lot less. If you know than speak with fewer words because the wax build up in the ears of most people only lets a little of the purity of truth enter in. Speak less and you will be more effective, if you know God. If you don't know God, you should listen to those around you who do.

If you understand that you are listening to a Self-Realized being, you would not be so casual about how you listen to them. Our priests cannot be ordained unless and until they are Self-Realized. You can't know what this is until you experience it, but it is necessary for one to be ordained a priest. A priest or teacher is one who stands in for God and mediates the divine presence. They are not to be adulated or worshipped, but they are worthy of the respect given to them because they have given their lives in service to human beings. They stand above the average humanity and know the way to take them to God. We are not kidding about this. We do stand between God and people and we take our job and our service seriously. We do no harm. We support all life. We are the handmaidens before the Lord. For those who have a concept that mediators are not necessary, I tell you that 2000 years of Jesus not being on earth has not made the earth a better place. Jesus came because God saw that we did, in fact, need a Mediator between human life and God. We were lost without some visual aid of what it looks like for God to manifest fully in a human being. So Jesus and Mary came in the flesh as perfect Masters to show us what perfection looked like and how it expresses. As a mass of people, we were not impressed and the world is going to hell in a hand basket ever since. What is it going to take for people to wake up to what they were given? How long do Jesus and Mary have to suffer the insults of such lack of respect and love? How many teachers have to give their life so that people wake up from their sleep?

You are here because you long for God. Let's face it. But don't get squeamish about how God wants to take you back home. We have the way, the truth and the life and we are successful with the willing in bringing them back to God as conscious sons and daughters of light. Will you let us teach you? Do you have the courage to give up your fears and your misconceptions? Can you stand letting someone love you and knowing you? Please come home and on the way maybe you will be able to enter into the service of helping others who want to come too.

About the Author:

Father Peter Bowes is a Christian Master Teacher. He has been teaching and training people on the spiritual path for many years. He brings people seeking real connection to God into the inner mystical teachings of Jesus and Mother Mary. He has directed various spiritual orders and now runs Ruach Center. Father Peter received his Masters and Doctoral degrees in Educational Psychology and ran a private psychotherapy practice for 20 years. He has authored many books including *The Word Within, Spiritual Astrology, The Radical Path, Pearls of a Fisherman, Love Is Simple, The Way, the Truth & the Life, Sayings of a Christian Master Teacher, The Joy of Stretching, a*nd the upcoming *Sermons from the Valley.* He has created many meditation recordings and has over 14 music CDs of devotional music and song. His music can be heard on iTunes and Amazon.